POETRY FROM THE FUTURE

'Ambiguous histories, temporal framings that do not
follow standard epochs, unexpected combinations of events,
are just some of the surprises and unsettlements that Srećko
Horvat gives us in this radically original book'
Saskia Sassen, author of *Expulsions*

'A charismatic Croatian philosopher' Oliver Stone

'One of the most exciting voices of his generation'
Das Freitag

'Thank fuck Horvat has taken it upon himself to create
new worlds' *VICE*

'The young Croatian philosopher Srećko Horvat is just as
much a doer as a thinker. He is searching for "the poetry from
the future" with impetuous energy' *Filosofie Magazine*

ABOUT THE AUTHOR

Born in 1983 in former Yugoslavia, Srećko Horvat is a European
philosopher without stable address. He is travelling across continents
giving lectures, visiting refugee camps and protests, and advocating
radical democracy as one of the founders and figureheads of the
Democracy in Europe Movement 2025 (DiEM25). He is the author of
numerous books, including *The Radicality of Love*, *What Does
Europe Want* (co-authored with Slavoj Žižek) and *Subversion!*

SREĆKO HORVAT

Poetry from the Future

PENGUIN BOOKS

PENGUIN BOOKS

UK | USA | Canada | Ireland | Australia
India | New Zealand | South Africa

Penguin Books is part of the Penguin Random House group of companies
whose addresses can be found at global.penguinrandomhouse.com

First published by Allen Lane 2019
Published in Penguin Books 2020
001

Copyright © Srećko Horvat, 2019

The moral right of the author has been asserted

Typeset by Jouve (UK), Milton Keynes
Printed and bound in Great Britain by Clays Ltd, Elcograf S.p.A.

A CIP catalogue record for this book is available from the British Library

ISBN: 978-0-141-98769-9

www.greenpenguin.co.uk

MIX
Paper from
responsible sources
FSC® C018179
www.fsc.org

Penguin Random House is committed to a
sustainable future for our business, our readers
and our planet. This book is made from Forest
Stewardship Council® certified paper.

The social revolution [. . .] cannot take its poetry
from the past but only from the future.
— Karl Marx, *The Eighteenth Brumaire
of Louis Bonaparte* (1852)

Contents

A Letter to the Future

Komiža
August 2018

This 'message in a bottle' was written on the remote Adriatic island of Vis, once famous as the headquarters of the Yugoslav Partisan struggle against the Axis powers in the Second World War, today probably better known as the imaginary Greek island in Mámma Mia! Here We Go Again. From here, far away from the mainland yet in the very heart of Europe, we could have seen the signs from the future approaching us like the Perseid meteors – or what we in Croatia call the 'tears of Saint Lawrence'.

But in these early August showers of shooting stars, so vivid against the island sky, we saw the sparks of our future as something which is a distant past, as a catastrophe that is already occurring, has already happened: devastating hurricanes, earthquakes, ravaging wildfires and record heatwaves across the globe; rampant authoritarian and right-wing regimes from Turkey to the United States, a lurch to the right in most European countries (Austria, Hungary, Italy, Poland, Germany), while the UK is stuck in the Brexit impasse of its own creation; massive displacements, with more than 68 million people fleeing war or persecution worldwide; new walls and new borders, detention camps for children; boats with refugees being rejected from our shores, with thousands drowning in the Mediterranean Sea; microplastics in our oceans, in the Antarctic and on Swiss mountains; climate change and the sixth wave of extinction (26,000 global species facing oblivion); the renewed threat of nuclear war and global geopolitical realignment; new developments in Artificial Intelligence and towards the colonization of Mars, along with dystopian sci-fi – The Leftovers, The Circle, The Handmaid's Tale, Westworld, *to name a few – which have become our dark documentary reality.*

Here, in the midst of this historic storm, life on Vis continues. Kajo and Jasna have finally built their house on the hill and my nephew swam for the first time in the Adriatic Sea; Pierce Brosnan enjoyed a brudet *(fish soup) in Komiža in a break from shooting* Mamma Mia! Here We Go Again, *while Vis's fishermen were returning from the nearby islands of Jabuka and Svetac with their haul. More and more tourists occupied the island every year; yet at the same time there was joy and hope, there were friendships and there was love; there was Čedo with his really existing utopia, warning us* Pazite preko semafora!* *or quoting Huxley's parrots: 'Attention! Here and now!', reminding us that the question of the future – our future – is being decided in every single moment. Maybe today, when you read this message, these snapshots of memories look like tiny grains of sand in the hourglass of time, but they are still mountains containing our yesterdays and tomorrows. It just depends on how you look at the hourglass.*

Smrt fašizmu, sloboda narodu!†

---

* 'Mind the traffic lights!' (there are no traffic lights on Vis)
† 'Death to fascism, freedom to the people' – antifascist slogan of Partisan Yugoslavia

PROLOGUE

The First Sound from
Occupied Europe

It is April 1944 and most of Europe is occupied.

Look at the map. You will see France, Austria, the Netherlands, Slovakia, Italy, Finland, Denmark, Belgium, Greece, Hungary, Poland and the Kingdom of Yugoslavia all under Nazi occupation, with puppet states installed in Croatia, Romania, Bulgaria and Norway. While German bombs are still falling over London, the RAF is carpet-bombing Berlin. The end of the Second World War is nowhere in sight. The Allied front in Italy is stalled and Nazi propaganda claims that its operations on the Eastern front in Russia have been abbreviated for tactical reasons. The Allied invasion of Normandy is still two months away: an ambitious hope. De Gaulle forms a new regime in exile and Hitler and Mussolini meet at Salzburg.

In early 1944 concentration camps are still operating and exterminating millions. French Jews are deported to Nazi Germany, the first Jews transported from Athens arrive at Auschwitz, and Adolf Eichmann travels to Hungary to oversee the deportation of much of that country's Jewish population to the same concentration camp. In the occupied Netherlands, Anne Frank writes her diary, until her arrest by the Gestapo that August. Soviet forces reached Majdanek near Lublin, Poland, in July 1944; only in January the following year would they liberate Auschwitz.

In the midst of this apocalyptic nightmare, Mount Vesuvius erupted in Italy. This was also the year in which *Casablanca* won three Oscars at the sixteenth Academy Awards; and when Benjamin Green, seeking a way to protect soldiers from sunburn, invented sunscreen. Around the same time, Donald Trump's father, Fred, was already working in real estate – building and selling houses, barracks and apartments for US Navy personnel, later expanding into middle-income housing for the families of returning veterans. Donald would be born two years later, in 1946.

In these months of early 1944, just before the liberation of Paris when it would have its première, Jean-Paul Sartre's dark existentialist play *No Exit* was being rehearsed in secrecy in the French capital. In the UK, Laurence Olivier was working on his *Henry V*, commissioned by Winston Churchill to boost British troops' morale, while Hitchcock returned to the UK to make two short propaganda films in French for the British Ministry of Information (*Bon Voyage* and *Aventure Malgache*). On the other side of the channel, at the same time, Pablo Picasso wrote a play, *Desire Caught by the Tail*, which was performed in the home of surrealist writer Michel Leiris, with Albert Camus (who was the director), Jean-Paul Sartre, Simone de Beauvoir, Georges Bataille, Jacques Lacan and Picasso himself reading some of the parts. The party continued after the play because those who remained after midnight had to stay until dawn because of the curfew. According to the historical accounts of this party, Sartre sang '*Les Papillons de nuit*' and '*J'ai vendu mon âme au diable*'.[1] As Picasso's crowd partied, Samuel Beckett, hiding from the Gestapo, joined the French Resistance, but continued to work on his last English-written novel, *Watt*, which he'd begun the previous year in Paris and which, he said, provided him with 'a means of staying sane'.

It is early 1944 and most of Europe is occupied.

Now imagine. In the middle of all this, with yesterday in ruins and tomorrow uncertain, you are listening to the songs of Bing Crosby, Vera Lynn and Judy Garland on the BBC's Overseas Service, when suddenly, completely unexpectedly, the melodies stop. The radio presenter, his voice tinny over the airwaves, announces, after five years of devastating war, what he calls 'the first sound from occupied Europe'.

'We present recordings from perhaps the most unusual voyage ever undertaken by a BBC war correspondent,' he says. 'They have just arrived from the Army Headquarters in Italy, but when and how they were made we cannot tell you, as we do not know that yet. The only thing we do know is that they were made by Denis Johnston, our correspondent in a country which the Germans claim is in their hands, in Yugoslavia.'

The announcer continues:

> Across the Adriatic Sea, throughout the once carefree hunting grounds for rich yachts along the Dalmatian coast and in the wild picturesque heights of Yugoslavia, one of the most heroic battles of this war is in progress today ... These people know what they are fighting for. They have absolute faith that they are right and in their ultimate fate. And it is a great and unique experience in this world of cynicism and divided loyalty to be among them and to be able to help them.[2]

For reasons of secrecy, the reporter could not specify any location, name or rank. All the listeners know is that the broadcast is taking place somewhere in occupied Europe, in the Adriatic. All they can hear is the sound of liberation.

This sound from a possible future, an emancipated world that had not yet reached other parts of occupied Europe – from Paris to Warsaw, Amsterdam to Vienna – was broadcast only once in April 1944. The recording was forgotten, left in a bunker for thirty years before being accidentally rediscovered in 1975 by two Sarajevo journalists. During the following two years, the pair painstakingly reconstructed the recording and its context: where it took place and when; who were the people singing and marching in the background, preparing Yugoslavia's liberation. Who the broadcaster was.[3]

At first, all the journalists had was the sound, the broadcast itself. Even in the BBC archives, the archivists knew only that the broadcast had been made in March or April 1944. Finally, however, the journalists managed to find the people behind the recording's voices and to reach the reporter, the Irishman Denis Johnston – a contemporary of Yeats and Shaw – who was still living in Dublin, and who told them the recording was the 'greatest professional challenge of his journalistic career'.[4]

Johnston also told them where the broadcast was made: the island of Vis, in the Adriatic Sea.

Who knows how many struggles of the past have been and will be forgotten, from original sounds to experiences and memories. The two journalists from Sarajevo succeeded not only in reconstructing a fleeting and long-forgotten event. They did something much more.

What they did was best explained by the German philosopher Walter Benjamin in his 1940 *Theses on the Philosophy of History*, written in occupied Paris, with a gas mask hanging on the wall above his writing table:

> To articulate what is past does not mean to recognize 'how it really was'. It means to take control of a memory, as it flashes in a moment of danger.[5]

This sound of a forgotten historic struggle which took place in the very heart of occupied Europe allows us not so much to understand how it really was, as to embrace the memory of that crucial historic moment when Europe trembled on the brink of liberation, to understand its unfulfilled potentialities – potentialities that are still relevant to our own present and crucially to building a better future. For us today, the most important lesson of the Yugoslav Partisan historical sequence lies in the fact that what started as a war, and turned into a world war, acquired the form of a revolution. Or to be more precise, the Partisans used the misfortune of occupation to mobilize the population in order to fight their way out of it. Instead of being victims of their historical circumstances, the Yugoslav people took control of them and turned them to their own advantage. From the mountains of Bosnia, Herzegovina and Montenegro, through the woods of Slovenia, Croatia and Serbia, and finally on the island of Vis, fighting a guerrilla war against the outnumbered Nazis and fascists – including the local collaborators, the Ustaša and Četniks – the Partisans succeeded not only in liberating the Yugoslav territory, but in establishing a new society based on the revolutionary struggle.

Today, when historical revisionism (the process of rewriting history and turning fascism into a legitimate discourse) and 'presentism' (the deluge of instant and fake news, and the world of social networks) are capturing every memory, we have to remind ourselves of Benjamin's words:

> The only writer of history with the gift of setting alight the sparks of hope in the past is the one who is convinced of this: that not even the dead will be safe from the enemy, if he is victorious.[6]

Today the enemy – whether it be the reinvention of fascism across the globe or the ongoing devastation caused by global capitalism (from austerity to the destruction of our planet) – is obviously victorious. The dead cannot be resurrected, but their deaths and sacrifices can acquire new meaning: if we are able to inscribe new resonance to the dead, if we can save their lives from oblivion and, more importantly, if we can liberate them from a current historical revisionist narrative and reality they themselves would not be ready to live with. The past (how it really was) is unfinished as long as we can fulfil its potential (how it really could be) in the future.

This is why this first sound picture from occupied Europe is so important. It is a glance not only into a short period of the past, it is a document of resistance, proof that there can be a resistance movement where, once again, there is occupation.

Occupation? Yes, occupation. The current occupation consists not only in the rise of fascist movements and authoritarian governments throughout the world; nor in the physical occupation of politics and space, with new walls and detention centres. It is also the psychical occupation of our emotions, desires and imagination, drowning in the melancholy and pessimism of the will. Our current occupation consists in the widespread sense – or even reality – that there is no alternative, and ultimately, that there is no future.

THE TOURIST 'OCCUPATION'

It is the start of summer 2017 and I am returning to the small island where this extraordinary broadcast took place.

Vis is one of the most remote inhabited islands in the Adriatic, and it takes more than two hours to reach it by ferry. Rising out of the sea, its scents of pine trees, carob, rosemary and oregano mingle with the smell of sea salt carried by the winds. As we drive through the hills of the island to reach the fishing village of Komiža on its western coast, the sound of crickets immerses us in a different way of temporality. Everything is slower here; imperceptibly, time starts to go into reverse. And the longer you spend here, the better you will get acquainted with the island's particular philosophy of life: *pomalo*. It is a greeting you might hear on the street ('take it easy') , or a casual answer you get when you want to make an appointment ('let's see'). But first and foremost it is a way of being.

And as always, for a short tranquil moment at the arrival of summer we can be certain that the ever-present sea will always be here, just like this, crystal clear and infinite. Whatever is happening in the world, whatever will happen, the sea will endure, with no end at the horizon, a reflection of our own transience.

But suddenly we are reminded that this summer season is ephemeral. We see aeroplanes 10,000 metres above us heading towards Italy. And every time we look at these distant white dots, we are relieved it is not us travelling in one of them.

Unlike the hordes of tourists who occupy Vis every year, however, we know life is hard here. Tourists who see my friend Senko Karuza – a poet and excellent chef – ordering his morning vodka with a slice of lemon probably think he's a quaint example of a local living the good life. But as he says, 'For me it is already evening!' He works in his vineyard from five in the morning, then heads to his *konoba* restaurant, where he cooks until he knocks off at midnight.

Tourists probably think the lady at the small grocery store must be crazy, because when, marvelling at the weather and the still, blue sea, they ask her whether she's been swimming recently, she says she hasn't done so for eighteen years. She's always happiest when the weather breaks because the heat makes work almost impossible, and the last time she went in the sea was when she was teaching her young daughter to swim. Now, she works relentlessly so her daughter can finish her studies and build a hopefully better future – which means leaving the island in order to find a job.

Every now and then, certain self-styled 'saviours' from Europe who descend on Vis try to convince these hard-working people that they are here to help them save the island. They recount examples of small villages and communities which Europe succeeded to 'save', where the locals have become successful working in the tourist industry, instead of slaving all day in the fields or fishing from early morning or all night. These people have, say the 'saviours', perfected the art of fulfilling the desires of the tourists, while preserving their culture, by opening 'ethno-villages' in which tourists can see how villagers still use traditional crafts. They don't understand that for our people an ethno-village is a sort of postmodern 'sustainable' zoo.

When I came to the island for the first time some ten years ago, there was still no mass tourism. Ironically, it was the Yugoslav People's Army (JNA), not Europe, which preserved the island, its traditions and untouched nature. From 1944 until the collapse of Yugoslavia in 1991 Vis was one of the strategically most important Adriatic army bases and no foreign visitors were allowed. Until the early 1990s it was untouched by tourism.

At one point Vis, with its ten factories, was producing 57 per cent of all the tinned fish of the Dalmatian coast. When communism collapsed the industry went too. Today, nothing of it is left due to 'structural adjustments' (the transition from communism to a free market economy), which were supposed to lead Croatia into a bright new future. All the factories were privatized, then went bankrupt, leaving workers without jobs.

Nowadays the only engine of the Croatian economy is tourism; the Croatian economy literally wouldn't exist without it. According to the 2016 statistics, Croatia has the highest tourist GDP in Europe: at 18 per cent of GDP it is far ahead of Italy (2.2 per cent) and Spain (4.7 per cent). The flip side of this tourist success story is a devastated economy. Where once there were factories, today we have only services.

The most recent structural adjustment of the never-ending transition from communism to capitalism is the Croatian conservative government's law that effectively paved the way for the privatization of the country's beaches. Back in the 1990s, after the dissolution of socialist Yugoslavia, everything in state or social ownership was privatized, from factories to telecommunications, from the oil company to the banks.[7] Given that there is barely anything left to privatize, it was just a matter of time before beaches and islands, the last public spaces, would become private as well. With 1,777 kilometres of coastline, 1,200 islands and around 2,000 beaches, Croatia is obviously an almost infinite reservoir for something which might soon become Europe's first private resort, turning the whole country into a sort of gated community.

A few years ago came a harbinger of this privatization. Tourists from Europe, mostly Swedes, started to descend on Vis every summer.

Some five or six hundred of them would come once a week in a fleet of thirty or forty sailing boats. Occupying the local beach bar, they would turn it into a typical western European disco, which of course is not free. The locals were unable to afford tickets to a beach which was until then free and public. Now the tourist boats come twice a week to Vis (which in a way is lucky, given that boats run daily to all the other Adriatic islands). Every day, more rubbish piles up.

Barba* Senko tells me that one of his friends, just back from watering olive trees in his drought-afflicted fields, came up with this idea for the tourists: instead of partying all night, each of them would be allocated an olive tree to tend. They could then buy all the olive oil which was produced from this tree and in return bask in the warm glow of their contribution to the sustainable development of the island. This is the future of tourism, he thinks.

Mostly, though, the people of Vis prefer to work their fields rather than dreaming of some new start-up. It's hard, but at least for a few hours they are alone and content. They don't want to be anyone's saviours. And above all, they don't want to be saved by their saviours.

THE FASCIST OCCUPATION

What the tourists and saviours don't know is a simple fact: here a stone is not merely a stone. Every stone is a document of resistance.

Every house, now turned into a *konoba*, *rakija*-bar or boutique hotel, was once a shelter for refugees, a hospital, a theatre, a radio office. Fields were once transformed into airports and sports grounds (cricket was and is still being played here); devastated buildings were factories; caves were illegal printing offices.

Long before the tourists, our small island in the Adriatic Sea was occupied for centuries. In the fourth century BC, the Greek tyrant of Syracuse, Dionysius the Elder, founded the colony Issa on the island. Later it became an independent *polis*, with its own money and even its own colonies. It was a Roman colony until the collapse of the Roman

* A Dalmatian (and Italian) word commonly used for older people of the local community

Empire, following which it was under the rule of the Republic of Venice for three and a half centuries, until 1797. After being handed on to Napoleon and then the Kingdom of Italy – with Italian as the official language – the island was ruled by the Austrian Empire for just over a century. Following the First World War, it was briefly Italian again. Finally, in 1920 it was ceded to the Kingdom of Yugoslavia.

During the Second World War, the island was occupied again, this time by fascist Italy. As Italian troops landed on 30 April 1941, locals lit bonfires on prominent hills and all the villages were daubed with antifascist graffiti.[8] Italian slogans were overwritten by local youths, who added *Vederemo* ('we'll see') to the Italian *Vinceremo* ('we will win'). The next day, the workers' holiday of 1 May, people flooded onto the streets in celebration – and in what was evidently a protest against the occupiers.

The fascists immediately set about trying to suppress resistance. The Italian language was imposed in schools and public institutions; all Croatian signs were removed from municipal buildings and replaced by portraits of Mussolini and Italian flags. Now, the official greeting was the notorious raised arm 'Roman' greeting. Closing the island's sports clubs and theatre groups, they opened their own: 'Fascio' for adults, 'Piccole' for the youth, 'Ballila' for children and 'Dopolavoro' (a famous ideology and practice invented by Mussolini back in 1926) for the post-work leisure of adults.

In a misperception common since time immemorial, what the occupiers didn't understand was that the local population would rather starve or die than live and serve under fascist occupation – or any other occupation, come to that.

As the Italians and Germans occupied most of the disintegrating Kingdom of Yugoslavia, many of Vis's young people left to join the Partisan resistance in the mountains and forests of Bosnia, Serbia, Croatia, Slovenia and Montenegro, while the rest of the population resisted the occupiers in all possible ways.

Workers in the island's sardine-canning factories, whose produce was now exported back to fascist Italy's armies, carried out acts of sabotage and subversion, from go slow strikes to using faulty packaging, and producing batches without preserving oil, or with the oil replaced by chemicals. The seasonal workers in the vineyards went on strike, prompting the rest of the island's seasonal workers to down tools as well.

The resistance took many forms. When, occasionally, the mines anchored in the sea came free from their moorings and were blown onto the island, fishermen would capture and dismantle them, turning them into hand grenades for the Partisan resistance movement.

There were other, similarly dangerous acts: on the anniversary of the October Revolution in 1942 a young Partisan called Nikola 'Top' Marinković, son of a poor fisherman, climbed to the top of the 50-metre-high bell tower of Komiža church and unfurled a red flag with the hammer and sickle. Although the young man managed to escape the ensuing volley of rifle fire from furious Italian troops, he was later killed. His act of courage was more than just a symbolic gesture of defiance. It was a sign from the future, a sign that liberation could be achieved if the other locals were prepared to show similar courage. And they did. Because courage is contagious.

With the resistance continuing, the Italian navy blockaded the island and started rounding up suspects. When people began to flee the villages and towns for the fields, hills and forests, the Italian occupiers imposed a general ban on movement, putting the entire population under house arrest. They detained ten suspected Partisans and shot them next to the church, while the locals, under house arrest, watched through the half-open windows. But this couldn't – and didn't – stop the resistance movement either.

When Mussolini's regime fell on 25 July 1943, the island's inhabitants started organizing for the final liberation. All over Vis, bonfires were lit, people flooded the beaches, singing Partisan songs. They took the island back.

THE LIBERATION OF THE ISLAND

Today, as the last participants in this historic struggle pass away and its memory fades, we reassure ourselves with the old mantra 'It can't happen here', or just indifferently look on while Europe is being occupied again by new forms of fascism or other dystopian nightmares under a name yet to come. On the one hand, Europe is already occupied by powerful financial institutions, banks and corporations which know no borders. Countries on the continent's periphery – Greece, Spain, Croatia – were the first victims of this 'shock therapy' (austerity, privatizations), but now the boomerang is returning to the centre: the UK, France, Germany, with new labour laws and market deregulation, including the privatization of healthcare, education and public spaces. *The Gilets jaunes* ('Yellow Vests') protests that hit France and Europe in late 2018 were a reaction to that, not to a simple increase in carbon tax; it was the victims of austerity who were protesting. On the other hand, many European states are either witnessing a rise of extremist and populist movements – the Alternative für Deutschland in Germany; France's Marine Le Pen – or a shift to radical right and xenophobic governments (Italy, Austria), or have already been transformed into semi-authoritarian states with new laws and changed constitutions (Hungary, Poland). New borders and walls are being erected, while the EU army sends patrols to its outer borders with Croatia and Albania, and to Mediterranean countries such as Libya where the refugee problem is being 'outsourced'.

On top of this, in June 2018 the hardline interior ministers of Austria, Germany and Italy formed what the Austrian Chancellor Sebastian Kurz called an 'Axis of the willing' to combat illegal immigration into the EU. His choice of phrase, coincidentally or otherwise, carries much darker historical undertones: a previous 'Axis' between precisely those three countries occupied Europe in the Second World War, with dire consequences for the whole continent and its people.

The question is not so much what the future of Europe will look like; it's more traumatic than that. What if the future is already here? What if Donald Trump's (or Poland's, Hungary's, Austria's) evangelic fundamentalism will lead us directly into the science-fiction autocracy of Margaret Atwood's *The Handmaid's Tale*? What if Europe's crisis will bring us into the nightmare of Alfonso Cuaron's dystopian movie *The Children of Men* (2006), in which the 'state of exception' (civil war, refugees in cages, terrorist attacks) has been normalized?

It is precisely in this context of what might be described as the beginning of a new 'occupation' of Europe that the story of Vis, a story from the past, resonates with potential for our future.

What the period of fascist occupation of Vis shows is that resistance can acquire many forms and even a small number of determined people on a remote and isolated island can defeat a numerically and technologically superior enemy. The period of liberation, meanwhile, shows that the flip side of resistance is – and must always be – the progressive, constructive part. Resistance to the old world and building a new one have to go hand in hand, simultaneously. A determined 'No' has to be followed by an even more determined 'Yes'.

Vis's history embodies this perfectly.

As soon as the local population liberated the island from the fascist occupation, the people returned to their villages, fields and ships. As the rules and laws of the fascist regime were abolished, people started collectively rebuilding what was destroyed, they returned to the fields and stored carob, figs and grapes for the struggle that would follow: the final liberation and foundation of Yugoslavia, whose starting point was Vis in 1944. When the island was liberated there was little money. It was a barter economy: fresh fish for meat, or eggs for bread. Cigarettes became available only when the Partisans broke into German warehouses on the mainland.[9]

And, as in the time of occupation, necessity became the mother of invention. When Vis, then the only liberated Adriatic island, was bombed by the Germans, the local fishermen watched where the bombs fell. If one exploded in the sea, as soon as the coast was clear, they would rush to collect the fish: massive catches of up to 100 kilos per explosion. The bombing was turned into an opportunity to feed the local population and its resistance movement.

In the last months of 1943, the British arrived, but even before then, Allied pilots operating out of Italian bases against Yugoslav, Austrian or Romanian targets had Vis inscribed in red on their flight maps: a friendly island British or American pilots could aim for in the event of an emergency. The British and the islanders set about transforming Vis into a frontline base, clearing 60 hectares of vineyards so that an airfield could be built on a site in the hills. Today, the airport is once again covered in vines, but the shape of the fields and the surrounding stones tell of the island's once-strategic importance.

The real revolution in these months, however, was the construction of a new society.

As a number of British spies, doctors and RAF officers would later recall, the biggest achievement of the period of liberation was that of self-government: all aspects of life were organized locally by the villagers themselves.[10] A people's committee was in charge of the economy and welfare of the whole community. What was more, every other village or town in the free territory of Yugoslavia would come to be organized along this model; the resistance movement, on the other hand, was led centrally. If we ever had the necessary dialectics between what activists today call 'horizontality' and 'verticality', it was here: democracy at its best.

The resistance not only radically transformed the economy but the very core of society. In 1944 an RAF officer described the island to Denis Johnston. 'You will like it here,' he said.

> It is the most incredible operation in first rows of struggle which I have ever seen. It is a strange army – men, women fight, live and work together. Kids, boys between 10 and 12, armed by hand grenades and rifles, work as couriers. More precise, they walk through the enemy lines, carrying messages from one partisan headquarters to the other. Men and women share responsibilities and duties equally – on the basis of complete equality. Discipline is strong. Flirting is extremely undesirable. Gender differences are, seems so, put ad acta until the war is finished. Some of the partisan women are incredibly handsome. They have an enchanting smile which puts a spell on you. But you can't misinterpret their cheerful *Zdravo*. They greet you as an ally, not as a potential boyfriend. After all, look at their equipment – girls with braids have machine guns, bayonets at their arms and two bombs, fastened to the strap. They are always armed, even when they dance.[11]

The officer clearly stared too long. He recalled a sharply humorous put-down from one of the partisan women, Katja: 'You Englishmen, you are so funny, you never look the girl in her eyes, you only look at her "bombs".'[12]

POETRY FROM THE FUTURE

Nowadays, with Vis overwhelmed by global capitalism and historical revisionism, ethno-villages and yacht weeks, consumerism and rubbish, selfies and drones, these echoes of resistance are faint indeed. But perhaps these reverberations offer us more than simply sounds from the past. Sitting on Vis, listening to the 1944 broadcast, I am not just transported into a historic moment that *was*. Being here, immersed in the sound of what took place here, I am present in that moment – and I get the feeling that, somehow, we might be able to project the spirit of this past struggle into the future.

This overlapping of two seemingly distant moments in time occurs in our present, in the here and now. So we are the ones who have the chance to connect them, to endow a past liberation struggle with a different form, not just by listening to it or reading about it but by a commitment – a commitment to changing the present and building a better future. Only a few years ago, if someone told you children would be filling detention camps in the United States and boats with exhausted refugees would be turned away from European ports, it might have sounded like a dark fantasy or the vision of an egregious pessimist. Today we are living in a long winter of melancholy, not only in Europe but across the world, a period in which the most important condition for shaping our future is evaporating – namely, hope: hope that anything other than this nightmare might be possible.

To explore the idea that this first sound from occupied Europe lives in the future and as such carries a message for our present, I am leaving the island for a short time: as a kind of archaeologist of the future who is determined to find signs leading us towards fulfilling its full potential. Not to repeat, but to construct something new, even if it has to be built in our current dystopian desert.

A morning which doesn't give birth to something new, as Senko would say, is a lost morning.

So, I am taking a boat to the continent.

A boat journey of a few hours doesn't really feel like travelling; more like being part of the island's daily rhythms. On the ferry, I meet people, mostly tourists returning from their well-deserved holidays to 'real life'. Both those who managed to relax and switch off and those who – much as they tried – didn't are becoming visibly tense with anticipation.

I can see it on their faces, in the irritable manner they treat their children or pets, in the way they start their car engines before the ferry docks. You can see it, above all, in the anxiety in their eyes. They know it's finished. This short, always too short, period of innocence and serenity.

After escaping the busy port terminal at Split, I reach the airport. It's packed, the floors of the departure terminals thick with people already one step back into their daily lives, immersed in post-summer melancholy. The summer finished too soon. Always too soon.

For many of us, there are no islands any more. Even if summer temporarily anaesthetizes us, dissolves our obsession with daily politics, deflation and recession, wars and terrorist attacks, climate change and refugee crises, it's all still present, lurking behind every stone.

For me, though, this isn't a return to 'real life', because reality is always already there, on Vis. The question is: how much reality? Nowadays, even on your remote island, you won't escape the banks and consumerism, Instagram or Facebook, supermarket chains and imported food, EU regulations and loans, tourists and rubbish. Capitalist realism has penetrated even the furthest islands. Yet somehow the view from the island enables you to see more clearly, to discern the sharp outlines of political, social and economic transformations which back in real life seem so natural, as if they were always there.

On the island we can see how starkly capitalism (with its structural adjustments and consumerist culture) and historical revisionism (with its ultimate desire to erase all memory not in line with the current official ideology) go hand in hand. As two sides of the same coin, they reinforce each other. Where there was a memorial site, today there stands a bank. Where there was a refugee shelter, now there's a restaurant. On the site of a factory is a 'rent-a-kayak'. It's not only Vis. Many small corners of Europe (in Spain, Greece, Italy and many other countries) have a similar wartime history of local resistance, of post-occupation reconstruction, of community.

While the fascist occupation imposed its language and rules by brute force, the current occupation achieves it through cultural hegemony that makes it impossible to do anything but accept the new order. And while Vis is commercialized and commodified in every aspect, the memory of its antifascist and emancipatory legacy is being erased, because if you remember or if you are able to speak a different language, you might come to the dangerous desire to resist. Remembering and speaking give birth to resistance.

In a world in which no one cares about the past any more, but no one has any hope in the future, the stones must start talking again. We ourselves, in this world of cynicism and divided loyalty, must become the first sound from occupied Europe.

Without forgetting the past struggles, our strength must come from the future. From that voice which might one day be rediscovered and which would be able to say with pure admiration and respect: these people knew what they were fighting for. They had the absolute conviction that they were right and had faith in their ultimate fate. And it was a great and unique experience to be among them and be able to help them.

PART ONE

The Sounds of Occupation

I

Summer in Hamburg:
Back to the Future

It is July 2017 and I am in Hamburg, where the G20, the biggest gathering of world leaders, is taking place. Hours ago I was surrounded by the perpetual concert of cicadas; now I'm shocked awake. Most of the main roads are blocked off and a militarized 'red zone' has been established in the city centre. More than 20,000 police, most heavily armed, patrol the streets, backed up by drones and the full range of surveillance technology. Helicopters are permanently parked in the clouds, the clatter of their rotors forming a continuous background music you soon learn to tune out. Constant police and ambulance sirens, emergency lights and water cannon accompany this orchestra of power.

To walk through the Hamburg streets in summer 2017 is a surreal experience. Although the city authorities promised not to ban the public demonstrations announced before the summit, just before its start they decided to issue a general decree forbidding any kind of assembly within a 38-square-kilometre range.[1] In practice this means that the centre of the city is completely blocked off and occupied, roads are empty and the red zone – where the summit is taking place – is surrounded by special forces, armed vehicles and roadblocks.

According to a poll just a few weeks prior to the summit, every third person living in Hamburg wanted to leave the city during the G20 summit. Hardly surprising: who would want to share their city with Trump, Erdoğan, Putin, Merkel and the Saudis, 20,000 policemen and an estimated 100,000 protesters? More to the point, why would anyone actively want to come to this hell?

Because the G20 in Hamburg 2017 – and the violence of a system determined to crush even symbolical resistance (only a few hundred protesters were violent) – or to be more precise, what it represents, might happen anywhere. If it's not happening yet in our own bubbles – on our islands, in our cities or countries, in our homes, within our families or in our safe circles of friends – it doesn't mean it hasn't already been happening for decades elsewhere in the world.

When the previous G20 summit took place the year before in Hangzhou, a city with over 6 million inhabitants, the Chinese government found a brilliant solution to the problem, one reminiscent of old communist times.[2] Weeks before the summit, it declared a week-long holiday and encouraged citizens to get out of town: 'If you don't like it, no problem, just leave the city!' Unlike the wise Chinese, some idiot must have pointed to the map of Germany and said, 'Let's hold the next G20 in Hamburg!' Given the city's strong leftist, anarchist and activist legacy, hosting the G20 was a recipe for trouble.

Signs of resistance are evident everywhere. Beside police checkpoints, there are huge billboards for the popular German cola (Fritz-Kola), depicting Donald Trump, Recep Tayyip Erdoğan and Vladimir Putin calmly sleeping – with the inscription *Mensch, wach auf!* ('Man, wake up!'). An obvious appeal to the politicians who have (supposedly) closed their eyes to global wars, terrorism, refugee crises and climate change, it was also a wake-up call to all citizens of Hamburg and beyond to organize and protest not only against the G20, but against the prohibition of protest itself.

Hamburg 2017 was a key historical moment when the leaders of the early twenty-first century, from Trump and Erdoğan to Putin and Xi Jinping, Merkel, May and Macron, gathered in one place at the same time. Though it might provoke the fleeting illusion that there is still something like a united and homogeneous G20 or global leadership, the current G20 rather resembles the young pope in Paolo Sorrentino's eponymous TV series. In *The Young Pope* Jude Law portrays the ultra-conservative and decadent Pius XIII, who drinks Zero Cherry Coke for breakfast, smokes in defiance of a Vatican smoking ban, and has serious doubts about whether or not he believes in God. In this similar situation, one of the traditionally most powerful economic and political blocs doesn't seem to believe in itself any more – as became clear in Hamburg that summer.

Whereas the old G20 was univocal in promoting and implementing either the old 'Washington Consensus', or the new 'Washington

Consensus'*, the new G20 can only agree to disagree. Likewise, while the previous G20 agreed on the meaning and practice of 'globalization', the current G20 is divided like never before. At the Hamburg G20, Angela Merkel was pushing for free trade, while Donald Trump stuck to his protectionism ('America First!').

Neither is there agreement among the expected allies, for instance between Germany and China. Ahead of the G20, the Chinese delegation visited Merkel in Berlin, and donated two giant pandas to the Berlin Zoo as a token of the friendship between the two countries. All this 'panda diplomacy' did was try to smooth over the fact that not even China and Germany can agree any more on the meaning of globalization. Or, as Merkel herself put it in front of the two giant pandas, 'Beijing views Europe as an Asian peninsula. We see it differently.'[3] The truth lies, of course, in the pandas. That's to say, China is already taking over Europe, not only through gifts of pandas but with smart investment and the biggest twenty-first-century infrastructure, transport and economic project called the 'One Belt, One Road' or the 'New Silk Road'.

Then there's climate change and Donald Trump's withdrawal from the Paris Agreement. Even if the rest of the G20 seemed united in distancing themselves from Trump, the G20 nations still provide four times more public financing to fossil fuels than to renewable energy. The 2017 escalation of conflict in the Middle East was another source of incongruity, with opposing global powers directly engaged in the Syrian conflict, or Western governments selling arms to those actively involved, gathered in Hamburg as the war in Syria raged on. Likewise, all the G20 nations at the summit pronounced themselves united in their 'fight against terrorism', then happily continued peddling lucrative arms deals that help create or prolong brutal wars and in the process fuel global terrorism. As the cherry on top of European democracy, the Saudis – with whom Trump in May 2017 sealed a weapons deal worth nearly $110 billion – were present at the G20 discussions,

---

* After the G20 summit in London 2009, where the world powers declared the Washington Consensus dead, while at the same time empowering a key institution involved in this economic policy, namely the IMF, by giving it $1 trillion in extra resources

block-booking the entire 165-room, thirty-one-suite Four Seasons Hotel, which, of course, was protected by heavily armed German police forces.[4]

There was something missing in the German cola wake-up ad. The problem is not that the leaders of the authoritarian world are asleep. They know perfectly well what they are doing – and they do it nonetheless. The real problem is the 'dogmatic slumber' (to use Kant's beautiful and succinct expression) of the so-called 'leaders of the free world', represented at the Hamburg G20 by Merkel, May and Macron. For decades, such leaders have pushed globalization and the Washington Consensus. Perfectly happy to condemn Trump's withdrawal from the Paris Agreement, they nevertheless fail to demand complete carbon divestment – the withdrawal of investment assets from companies involved in extracting fossil fuels – which would redirect energy investments from unsustainable fossil fuels into clean and renewable energy. Meantime, they are also calling for new global internet regulations that would further restrict basic human and digital rights (free speech, the right to privacy, free internet and so on). Last but not least, most of the world's top ten arms-exporting countries (United States, Russia, France, Germany, China, United Kingdom, Italy)[5] gathered in Hamburg together with the world's largest arms importers (India, Saudi Arabia, Australia, Turkey) amid the usual rhetoric of global stability and peace.

These cynical contradictions were exposed on the first day of the G20 summit. While the whole city was blocked and empty and the protesters clashed with police in the neighbourhood of St Pauli, the world leaders were enjoying Beethoven's *Ode to Joy* in Hamburg's Elbphilharmonie, one of the world's largest and most acoustically advanced concert halls, presumably tuning out the words: 'Our magic joins again, what convention strictly divides, all people become brothers, where your gentle wing abides.'[6]

These famous lines offered an ironic commentary on the summit: the world's leaders divided among themselves; the people looked upon fearfully, as enemies. I joined a crowd of activists and Hamburg citizens marching towards the Fischmarkt at the city's port, where a public demonstration was taking place. On the other side of the Fischmarkt, a phalanx of heavily armed police and two mobile water cannons blocked the main road, the Elbstrasse; all surrounding streets were blocked. The police tactics were clear: shut off the rear exit and force the demonstrators to walk in the opposite direction, where they would be stopped by other officers and effectively 'kettled'.

As the crowd moved towards the one remaining exit, somewhere in its midst appeared members of the anarchist 'Black Bloc', in their black clothes and masks. In a sort of self-irony, this group – mainly young people in their early twenties – started to inflate a large black blimp, which was supposed to represent the Black Bloc. The others were equipped with small plastic bricks.

The police didn't have any sense of irony. By the time members of the Black Bloc had walked some 300 metres back towards the closed-off part of Hamburg, they were trapped between officers on one side and a riverside wall on the other. The police weren't interested in de-escalating the situation. Neither, however, did they want to make any arrests. In what was a transparent public warning to would-be demonstrators, members of the Black Bloc were singled out and beaten; everybody else present was subjected to teargas and water cannon. In response, stones and missiles were hurled at the police. As usual, the authorities, echoed by the mainstream media, portrayed everyone who was that evening at the Fischmarkt as violent rabble. The violence – a foreseeable reaction to police brutality– was inevitably described as 'incomprehensible'.

When, back in 2013, the Turkish prime minister Erdoğan ordered the ejection of protesters in Istanbul's Gezi Park claiming that 'terrorists' were infiltrating the ranks of demonstrators,[7] European leaders were quick – as they always are when others have to be taught about 'democracy' – to condemn this crackdown and praise the democratic values of assembly and freedom of opinion. Yet what happened four years later in Hamburg was remarkably similar. Although most of the anti-G20 demonstrations and events were peaceful, the system – using the legal notion of the 'state of emergency' (a situation of national danger or disaster in which a government suspends normal constitutional procedures in order to preserve or regain control) – reduced the diverse and heterogeneous assembly to what the German press described as just a 'bunch of militants'.

Over the past couple of decades, more or less since 9/11, the state of emergency has long ceased being the exception; now, indeed, it has more or less become the rule. After the Paris terrorist attacks of November 2015, the French government declared a state of emergency which is still in place today. In order to protect the French people from the threat of terrorism, the state imposed hundreds of unjustified measures restricting freedom of movement and the right to peaceful assembly. According to Amnesty International, between November 2015 and May 2017 the French authorities used emergency powers to issue 155 decrees prohibiting public assemblies, in addition to banning dozens of protests using ordinary French law. They also imposed 639 measures preventing specific individuals from participating in public assemblies. Of these, 574 were targeted at those protesting against proposed labour law reforms. According to media reports, the authorities imposed dozens of similar measures to prevent people from participating in protests after the second round of the presidential elections on 7 May 2017.[8] Peaceful protest is seen as a potential threat, rather than a fundamental right. Similar states of emergency have recently been put in place – or still are – in various European states, including Italy, Germany, Spain, Belgium, the United Kingdom and Turkey.

The Hamburg G20 was not only a temporary state of emergency. Rather, because of the other states of emergency across Europe and the world, it comes closer to the notion of 'state of exception' (*Ausnahmezustand*), defined by the legal theorist Carl Schmitt as the right of the sovereign to transcend the rule of law in the name of the public good. In other words, in order to defend the constitution, the constitution can be suspended. In order to protect the people, it is the people's fundamental rights – freedom to assemble, protest and so on – which are suspended first.

Indeed, the concept of the state of exception is so tightly woven into the history of Germany between the two world wars that it is impossible to understand Hitler's rise to power without understanding the uses and abuses of Article 48 of the Weimar Constitution.*

---

* Article 48 reads: 'If security and public order are seriously disturbed or threatened in the German Reich, the president of the Reich may take the measures necessary to reestablish security and public order, with the help of the armed forces if required. To this end he may wholly or partially suspend the fundamental rights.'

The last years of the Weimar Republic were acted out in a state of exception. As the Italian philosopher Giorgio Agamben points out in his book of that name, Hitler's rise to power might not have been so straightforward had Germany not been under a regime of presidential dictatorship for nearly three years and had parliament been functioning. The situation in which Germany found itself in the last moments of the Weimar Republic was justified by Schmitt on a constitutional level by the idea that the president acted as the guardian of the constitution, but the end of Weimar clearly demonstrates that, as Agamben says, a 'protected democracy' is no democracy at all: the paradigm of constitutional dictatorship functions instead as 'a transitional phase that leads inevitably to the establishment of a totalitarian regime'.[9]

In this light, maybe the renewed recent interest in the years of the Weimar Republic isn't just a coincidence. Let's look at the popular German TV series *Babylon Berlin*, based on Volker Kutscher's detective novel set during the decadence and disintegration of the late Weimar Republic and Germany's slide into Nazism. There is a direct connection between the cocaine dealers, pornographers, nationalists and criminals, the street battles between the police and the workers in *Babylon Berlin* with the state of exception and rising Nazism. And if we go back to the future, what if a better parallel to our own era isn't so much the 1930s (now frequently used to warn of the times ahead), but the 1920s and the period of Weimar? What if it's the state of exception deployed during its last years that carries a crucial lesson for our future?

As the images of Hamburg burning spread around the world, all attention was focused on the violence itself rather than its true cause, which was – alongside the policies of the G20 and the world order it represents – the state of exception imposed on the city. A day after the summit ended, the German tabloid *Bild* ran a cover with an image of black-clad protesters against a wall of flame under the headline: 'The hatred of the left can't be stopped. The guerrilla tactics of the G20'. The article concluded that 'not even 20,000 police could stop the incomprehensible escalation of violence'.[10] Even by its own long tradition of denouncing any sort of popular protest against the status quo, *Bild* excelled itself: it was this image that stuck in the popular imagination and which for governments and the mainstream media has continued to define the Hamburg summit.

The German foreign minister Sigmar Gabriel painted a picture of hordes of European activists converging on the city, hungry for violence, and compared them to 'neo-Nazis and their fire attacks'.[11] German politicians of almost all political stripes called for a Europe-wide extremism database, which one newspaper described as a show of 'rare bipartisan unity in Germany'.[12] What happened in the aftermath of the G20 conforms precisely to Agamben's description of a prolonged state of exception; indeed, it has resonances with Philip K. Dick's *Minority Report*, where the job of special forces is to stop a crime before it even happens. Today, obviously, the 'crime' is protest itself.

Extensive international anti-protest legislation already existed before the Hamburg G20. In events of similar global significance, activists were banned from entering Germany – the Kurdish leader Salih Muslim landed in Hamburg but was forced to return to Turkey – or were detained after visiting the G20. This happened to Eleanor Jones, who was detained at Edinburgh airport under schedule 7 of the Terrorism Act 2000 because she had attended the Hamburg protests. Forced to hand over her mobile phone and computer passwords, she was interrogated about the political beliefs of her relatives (including the *Guardian* columnist and political activist Owen Jones), following which she was taken to a police station to have a DNA sample and fingerprints taken.[13]

Now, with a Europe-wide extremism database or similar international activists' register, we could imagine that those tens of thousands of activists who were protesting – mostly peacefully – at the G20 in Hamburg could be prevented from entering particular countries where world powers gathered to discuss, seal or sell our future. And there's more: an algorithm, based on data harvesting, might decide that it knows who wants to protest at particular events before the protest in question even takes place. Pre-emptive politics will become the prevailing form of politics in the twenty-first century. If pre-emptive policing already draws on algorithmic prediction, what is the future of protest? And what is the point of traditional forms of protest if the real power doesn't lie in the armed vehicles or police helicopters, but precisely in the untouchable space of algorithms? What if the place where power truly resides is not in the material and visible, but precisely in the invisible, in digital surveillance and control?

It is here that we need to stop for a moment and undertake serious reflection on what actually happened in Hamburg if we want to answer one of the most important political questions of our time: are violent protests really so incomprehensible? From slave rebellions to revolutions, isn't such violence typically a reaction to the structural violence of a system that in the first place creates the conditions of humiliation, exploitation and despair? Obviously, the answer to the question of violence depends on which side you choose to sit, either with the system or against it. But the strategic question for progressive politics, if it wants to go beyond the violence, remains the following: how can we find a way of creating a real alternative to the current state of exception, a radical alternative that wouldn't be merely reduced to violent outbursts that create an even more violent reaction from the system (prolonged state of exception, surveillance capitalism, normalization of army on the streets)?

If anything was clear from what happened in Hamburg, it is that the three current models of resistance to global capitalism and the renewal of fascism – alter-summits, public demonstrations, violent protests – are no longer enough. If they ever were.

Alter-summits. These big international gatherings of progressives from across the globe (ranging from the radical left to greens, from trade unions to feminist movements) meet to discuss and exchange ideas, but simply don't have the capability to call into question the policies of major global powers or a power bloc such as the G20 or the World Economic Forum (WEF). While these counter-summits are necessary, they don't in themselves have the authority and agency needed to provide an alternative to global capitalism. One of the most successful alter-summits in the twenty-first century was undoubtedly the World Social Forum (WSF), founded in 2001 to counter the World Economic Forum, an annual gathering of powerful corporate and political elites held in Davos, Switzerland. The first WSF, with its roots in Latin American activism, was held that year in Porto Alegre (the city of the Workers' Party of future Brazilian president Lula da Silva). There was much hope at the beginning – best embodied in its famous slogan 'Another World is Possible!' – and throughout the next decade the WSF quickly grew and attracted more than 100,000 participants annually. For many progressives, it was the hope that the early twenty-first century could witness the birth of a genuine transnational global movement building a real alternative to neoliberalism. But slowly the number of participants declined. In August 2016, only 35,000 activists attended the twelfth World Social Forum in Montreal, Canada. There are many reasons for this. One is certainly the changed political situation in Latin America (including Brazil, where in 2018 Lula was imprisoned); another is the NGO-ization of the WSF and the lack of resources. Perhaps the most significant reason is that one of the most important principles of the WSF is that no one can ever speak 'in the name of' the Forum. Participants can speak for their organizations, possibly together with others, but not 'as Forum'.

Back in 2011, as the World Social Forum gathered in Dakar, Senegal, the 'Arab Spring' was unfurling across North Africa. I remember long meetings of social movements, intellectuals and activists from across the world. But instead of sending a unified message of support to the demonstrators, the International Council of the WSF, mindful of preserving the diversity and heterogeneity of its membership's views, did not send a joint communiqué or start a global action of solidarity and mobilization. And this is precisely the problem with alter-summits and forums: their ability to challenge the system is blocked by the fetish of horizontality (no hierarchies, self-management and the democratic participation of all) and the fear of speaking in the name of (a vertical decision-making structure with the capacity for efficient action). Yet such verticality is necessary if you want to question the system.

Public demonstrations. While massive public demonstrations often catch the media's attention, they do little more than enact dissatisfaction with the current global system. Governments find it all too easy to ignore the presence of even millions on the streets. In February 2003 over 10 million people protested in 600 cities simultaneously against the impending Iraq War. Their efforts, unfortunately, didn't stop it. So why would any another protest, of whatever scale – let's say against the wars in Libya, Syria or Yemen – have a different outcome? Unless public demonstrations are part of a deeper and structural organization capable of moving beyond large one-day events, their power remains purely symbolic.

Violent protests. Such protests start from the presupposition that peaceful public demonstrations are not enough to bring about change. The violence which usually erupts at big summits like the G20 tends primarily to be a reflection of the systemic violence which is the real problem. Nevertheless, even if violent protest reveals the brutality of the system, it is, again, not sufficient to challenge existing power structures, to create a real counter-power.

The contradictory nature of violent protest is somewhat unexpectedly encapsulated in the documentary film *Mein liebster Feind* (*My Best Fiend*, 1999) about the tense and complex relationship between the German film director Werner Herzog and the legendary actor Klaus Kinski.*

Kinski was often portrayed as crazy. He had a famously explosive temper, and at one point actually attempted to kill Herzog. But if we look at testimonies from the five movies Herzog and Kinski made together, a different picture begins to emerge, one in which, far from being crazy, Kinski's behaviour was pretty normal in the circumstances. If anything it is Herzog who comes across as mad: his 1982 film *Fitzcarraldo* being a case in point. It involves a crazy, determined Irish guy who wants to build an opera house in the middle of a jungle and involved Herzog in emulating his quixotic subject, hefting a three-storey 320-ton steamer from one river to another, across a muddy Peruvian jungle hillside in tropical 40-degree heat. Though he managed the feat, half the film crew were injured in the process. At least he had enough self-awareness to proclaim himself the 'Conquistador of the Useless'.

Ten years earlier, Herzog's movie *Aguirre, the Wrath of God,* starring Kinski, had also been filmed in the Peruvian jungle. Frustrated at the film crew's lethargy, Kinski fired a gun at them when they were playing cards. Subsequently, he attempted to leave the location, changing his mind only after Herzog threatened to shoot first Kinski and then himself. Remarkably, the pair's relationship lasted until the 1987 movie *Cobra Verde.* During the shooting of the film Kinski would have such fiery outbursts that none of the crew could stand 'the wrath of Kinski' any more. This explosive situation famously

* I owe this elaboration to Tonči Valentić (Croatia)

culminated in the film's original cinematographer, Thomas Mauch, walking out on the project after a torrent of verbal abuse from Kinski. The friendship between the actor and Herzog came to an end. Almost as though his life had been sustained by the creative violence of their relationship, Kinski died only four years later.

There is here an important political lesson about the meaning of violence. The real question is not why did Kinski behave like a madman, but why was Herzog so calm during his violent outbursts?

The answer is revealed in *Mein liebster Feind*, when in a quarrel with the producer Walter Saxer, Kinski wildly jumps and shouts like a madman. Herzog later said that he didn't want to intervene in this quarrel because, apparently, Kinski was in fact much calmer than usual. But at the end, one of the Peruvian film crew said to Herzog: 'You probably figured out we were scared, but at no point were we afraid of that screaming fool. We were actually afraid of you, because you were so silent!' And this is the reason why we shouldn't regard Kinski as the one who was crazy, but Herzog himself, who at the end of this whole adventure, when asked what he felt when he looked back on it, simply answered: 'Nothing!'

Taking into consideration the crazy conditions of Herzog's film-making, Kinski was in fact articulating a perfectly legitimate fear (how to carry a 320-ton steamboat through the jungles of Peru), while Herzog stayed calm. Maybe the reason was that Herzog was still, even under those circumstances, in control of his filmic world, a vision in which the helpless Kinski was subsumed.

When we are confronted with scenes of violence in Hamburg, or any other place where power assumes material form and is confronted, shouldn't we perceive the protesters as those who resemble Kinski, with their many legitimate reasons to be violent, and the systemic violence as Herzog, the one who will calmly answer back with greater brutality and the usual 'There is no alternative'?

Of course, Herzog is a brilliant film-maker who constantly subverts the system, but the point is – and this is precisely the reason why he is successful – to proceed in the calm conviction of your cause, because you know that, after all obstacles have been overcome, it will be realized. Or if not – at least you've tried.

Nevertheless, these three models of resistance remain crucial for one particular reason which could be called 'political subjectivation', the process of acquiring a political subjectivity through the experience of organizing and protesting, of confronting the system and one's own contradictions, and last but not least, of sharing comradeships and friendships across identities and borders, this feeling of togetherness which is able to create new spaces inside/outside of power.

From the G8 summits of Seattle (1999) and Genoa (2001), to Syntagma Square in Athens (which triggered the Greek Spring) and Puerta del Sol (which led to the rise of Podemos in Spain and the municipalist movement Barcelona en Comú), these uprisings open the way for what the French philosopher Michel Foucault labelled 'heterotopia' (literally, 'other place') or what the anarchist thinker Hakim Bey calls 'temporary autonomous zones'.[14] For Foucault, a heterotopia is the other or different space (from the ancient Greek *heteros*): intense, contradictory and transformative, both for those inside it and for society as a whole. Such spaces of resistance are not utopias (a world outside of this world), but worlds within worlds: realities which can turn worlds, values and desires upside down and will surely form an integral part of all struggles to come. At the same time, these are spaces of different temporalities (*pomalo*, for instance). The examples Foucault provides, among many others, are boats, brothels, cemeteries, gardens and prisons. We should add with regard to the Hamburg G20 or the huge demonstrations against Donald Trump in London in the summer of 2018, protests and massive mobilizations can – and should – also be a heterotopia.

We who are crazy enough to come from all corners of the world to a city occupied by Trump, Erdoğan, Putin, Merkel, the Saudis, drones and 20,000 policemen, we already form a heterotopia. On the last day of the G20 summit, Hamburg was transformed into such a heterotopia. As the world leaders departed, some 80,000 people gathered in a peaceful demonstration in the reopened city centre. Present were activists and ordinary people, children, the elderly, Kurds, Greeks, people from all nations and those without a nation; trade unionists, feminists and even the Black Bloc; united in marching and dancing, singing and celebrating this massive heterogeneous but at least temporarily unified world of protest.

Yet how can we move from this temporary heterotopia to

something more radical? How can the world within the world change the world? How can the values and desires of the heterotopia become the building blocks for a different world?

With these questions forming in my mind, I leave the demonstration, saying goodbye to my marching and singing comrades. We'll meet again, in other cities, other countries, in streets and at assemblies, everywhere there is resistance to the current dystopia. This was the lesson I carried away from Hamburg. A new world can be built only if we are aware that we have to invent new forms of protest and organization, together with new forms of political subjectivity. To put it like this: it's notable that during mass demonstrations, the left still sings twentieth-century songs of resistance. They are beautiful and important songs which shouldn't be forgotten, but if we want to create a truly new political subjectivity, we need new songs. Metaphorically and literally.

On my way to the airport I briefly stop in a suburb and see what I didn't see before. It already looks as if nothing happened: as if the events of the last few days might have been a dream. The shops are open and people are calmly going about their daily lives and routines. Everything seems normal. Only the headlines in the newspapers tell us that we're leaving a war zone. Instead of reporting the massive peaceful demonstration, the front-page images are of burning cars and violent clashes with the police. 'Merkel condemns "brutal" Hamburg protests,' blares the *Financial Times*.[15] 'Trump cheers safety at G20 despite the anarchists,' trumpets another paper.[16] President of the EU Commission Jean-Claude Juncker, meanwhile, pronounces that Hamburg had been the best location for the G20. Truly, a parallel reality.[17]

On the boat's deck, as I leave the mainland of Croatia and with it, Europe, the dystopia feels remote. This morning I was still surrounded by police and helicopters. Now, a full moon illuminates the infinite sea and my way home.

2

The Circle of Machinic
Enslavement

I'm disorientated, sure that I can hear the clatter of helicopters again. Then, as I surface, waking more fully, I realize where I am. Luckily, it's a July morning on Vis.

So, I go to the beach. The sun is high and the sea infinite, and I'm slowly sinking once more into the summer slumber. But there's that sound again. I look around me, confused – and there it is. A drone, high above the beach.

The Adriatic islands were dragged into this technological present some years ago. After the 1991 fall of Yugoslavia, when the Yugoslav People's Army (JNA) left Vis, the island became better connected to the mainland. Soon, we were embracing the newest technologies around the same time as everyone else in Europe: the first mobile phones and the internet in the late 1990s; Myspace and Trip Advisor in the early 2000s. What is the point of having a holiday from heaven, if you can't share it with others? What's the point of your enjoyment if no one can see it or like it? Then, in the early 2010s, came Facebook and Airbnb. As jobs and industry began to dry up, the locals realized that the one thing at least they could do was to rent out their houses and apartments for the summer.

Now it is drones. Usually they're used by a few wealthy tourists who, instead of venturing onto the 'dangerous' island from their expensive and safe yachts, use their drones to get a taste of real life on the island – and, given that there's no regulation, they can do so with impunity. We could imagine that in some near future it will be the state itself which uses drones to monitor and control remote islands. Or, if we pursue this idea to its logical conclusion, why not a corporation that has efficient tools to control and program everything, from emotions to elections?

By weird coincidence, that day our local open-air cinema was showing a movie from the future, a movie which concerned precisely such a universe. So I decided to go to the cinema to see what our future might look like.

The film opens with a girl in a kayak, in the sea. As the water gets choppy and the waves get higher, she paddles on and on. Relentlessly, through the restless sea.

The movie is based on Dave Eggers's speculative science-fiction novel *The Circle*. Written back in 2013, in an age when – believe it or not – the US president didn't have his own Twitter account, it's set in a hypothetical near future, a future in which a technology company called the 'Circle' becomes the most influential organization in the world.

The Circle has acquired the existing giants of Silicon Valley: Google, Facebook and Twitter. By creating a monopoly, the Circle gains total control over the lives and thoughts of humankind. In order to maintain this hold on humanity, it invents TruYou, an online identity based on all our online interactions (chats, emails, social media, business transactions, etc.) with each user having only one password and one identity for all internet activities ('one button for the rest of your life online'). All the data is, of course, stored in the cloud. Since TruYou eliminates pseudonyms and anonymous activity, it also restores real-life accountability to online comments and interactions. People are nicer. Shopping is easier. Communicating is quicker. People send 'zings'. They respond with 'smiles' or 'frowns'.

Or as the girl from the kayak, who would soon climb to the top of the Circle, reasons:

> If you care about your fellow human beings, you share what you know
> with them. You share what you see. You give them anything you can.
> If you care about their plight, their suffering, their curiosity, their right
> to learn and know anything the world contains, you share with them.
> You share what you have and what you see and what you know.[1]

As the next logical step, the Circle introduces a new technology called 'SeeChange' that allows users to place tiny cameras anywhere they like and share the footage with all others. At the beginning it is useful to view nature or traffic conditions, but soon these devices become important in holding governments accountable, especially in countries going through upheaval or revolution.

More and more elected officials all over the world go transparent. Those who don't, begin to feel pressured because it looks as if they are hiding something. As the imposed mantra says: 'SECRETS ARE LIES – SHARING IS CARING – PRIVACY IS THEFT'. Politicians who challenge the Circle end up on the news days later being arrested for criminal online activity. Meanwhile, 90 per cent of Washington goes transparent in a process called 'Clarification', leading to 'Completion', a totally transparent society. All vices and all crimes are to be eradicated by a technologically supported quasi-theology. Everyone is like god, omniscient, all-seeing; everyone is afraid of the eyes of all the other gods. It is a perfect Panopticon in which everyone is at the same time guardian and prisoner.

Although they raise awareness about the developments of Silicon Valley, the themes in Dave Eggers's novel aren't especially new – indeed, they weren't when it was written. What the book did do was follow the currents in Silicon Valley to their logical conclusion: total monopoly. In doing so, it presaged Peter Thiel's notorious dictum 'Competition is for losers!'[2]

The next logical step after creating a monopoly of the means of production (the physical facilities and resources for producing goods) is to monopolize the means of mental production (that which produces how we think, perceive, feel, act). This, of course, is what totalitarian systems have always done: first taking hold of the material infrastructure, then surveilling the population and analysing data in order to program behaviour (so-called 'biopolitics').

In this respect, too, you might say that *The Circle* is simply an early twenty-first-century iteration of a story written many times in the last century, most notably Yevgeny Zamyatin's 1921 dystopian novel *We*.

We portrays a world in which everything is transparent and everyone lives in the 'One State', an urban nation constructed almost entirely of glass. You can request an hour's privacy per day – to have sex, for instance – but only on condition that you inform the authorities of the exact time of intercourse and register your sexual partner.

Everybody wears uniform and is given a number. The main character is a spacecraft engineer called 'D-503' (in an echo of which, the main character of George Lucas's eponymous movie from the 1970s was THX 1138). The behaviour of all individuals is based on a logic outlined by the One State by way of equations and formulas. Every hour in one's life is directed by the 'Table'.

At first sight there is not much fundamental difference between *The Circle* and Zamyatin's novel: both describe a single state (the Circle, One State); both rely on total transparency (in Zamyatin's work glass is the metaphor, in the Circle it is SeeChange). The only difference is that Zamyatin was imagining a communist totalitarian regime – *We* was the first work banned by the Soviet censorship bureau Goskomizdat, with the author eventually allowed to emigrate to Paris in 1931 – while *The Circle* describes a capitalist one. Allegorizing an increasingly stringent Soviet government, Zamyatin wrote of the 'Great Operation' in order to prevent possible riots and remove emotions and imagination from the citizens of One State. Eggers introduces the process of Clarification, which will lead, finally, to the totally transparent society.

What really distinguishes the One State from the Circle, though, is that in the latter the citizens passionately desire the new order. They want transparency over privacy. They want their children protected and monitored, their education evaluated. They want their healthcare information centralized. And unlike in the One State, where citizens can't wait to hide for at least one hour a day and have sex, in the Circle most believe everything, even sex, should be transparent. They want to be surveilled, they want their steps and calories to be counted. They want drones hovering above the beaches.

In short, thanks to the developments of Silicon Valley, we've reached a moment which Zamyatin probably couldn't have dreamt up in his wildest imagination.

George Orwell began writing his *Nineteen Eighty-Four* some eight months after he read a French translation of *We*; indeed, he acknowledged that Zamyatin's book was a model for his own. Yet the conclusion of *Nineteen Eighty-Four*, a radical departure from *We*, was that people had started to love Big Brother.

Though it follows in the footsteps of earlier dystopian novels, what

The Circle offers is a new reading of the same topic (totalitarian transparent societies), applying it to the logical next steps and development of Silicon Valley. Knowing the beast from the inside: describing the campus of the Circle – which strongly resembles the headquarters of Google and Apple – and imagining how already existing technologies could be even more interconnected and integrated into a complex system governed by a monopoly instead of by competing companies, Eggers makes a far-reaching point: that politics itself will become preprogrammed; politics will become dependent on the algorithm which will know everything about you.

Eggers invites us to pose the following question: what if traditional nation-state politics is finished, what if Silicon Valley (or any technological company) acquires the role of the state or what if everything that we used to know as public (not only healthcare or education but voting itself) becomes privatized? This is where the Circle gets interesting.

At the Concept Kingdom meeting, a regular gathering at which the newest Circle technologies are announced, one of the company's founders (played in the movie by Tom Hanks) introduces a new concept that would increase democratic participation by automatically registering those with Circle profiles and then taking all voting to the same online platform. As he talks, the kayak girl, whose name is Mae, raises her hand and suggests that in order to increase voting participation the government might require all citizens of voting age to have a Circle account.

The speaker interrupts her, enumerating other things that are required by law and discussing the feasibility of freezing members' profiles until they have voted. The meeting ends with one attendee pointing out that the United States may not even need a Congress now that the will of the people can be determined so quickly and directly. In the end, the Circle introduces 'Demoxie', a new technology that allows – or, rather, forces – all citizens to vote through their TruYou accounts, which link access to government services not only to public records but also to users' online profiles.

One of the company's founders sees this technology as an opportunity to perfect electoral democracy, to close the circle between electors and elected. 'As we know here at the Circle,' he says to applause, 'with full participation comes full knowledge. We know what Circlers want because we ask (. . .) if we observe the same model nationally, electorally, then we can get very close, I think, to 100 per cent participation. One hundred percent democracy.'[3]

Mae, though, suggests taking things a step further. Why not, she proposes, oblige everyone to vote? 'Everyone would agree that 100 per cent participation is the ideal.' Until the requested vote has been cast, a Circle account will simply be blocked. 'And then we can take the temperature of everyone at any time.' The developers at the Circle are so excited that within a week they have a beta version of Demoxie – 'It's democracy with your voice, and your moxie. And it's coming soon.'

This is the perfect dystopia of the Circle: instead of just holding governments accountable by total transparency, everyone becomes part of the omnipresent and transparent new mode of capitalism. Not only do citizens give up their privacy, but they also give up the traditional model of political representation. Of course, we know very well that 'representative democracy' has many flaws – the worst form of government except for all others, as Churchill put it – but is this version of 'direct democracy' really better? Instead of governments, what we have here is Silicon Valley as the world direct democratic government. Instead of politics, we have algorithmic management.

Although Silicon Valley companies haven't yet accomplished what TruYou did, we are already giving up freely vast amounts of data (emails, location data, photos, chats, eating habits, sexual preferences, desires and dreams) to various internet companies, which is almost instantly hyper-integrated into a monopoly controlled system.

As ever greater quantities of data are stored and integrated through various interdependent technologies and services, while we may not yet have a 'smart party', Silicon Valley (Google, Facebook, Cambridge Analytica and so on) is already influencing the outcomes of elections. Only a few years ago, it would have sounded outlandish to say that elections could be manipulated by Big Tech. But with the 2016 Wiki-Leaks revelations (in the 'Podesta emails') it was out in the open that Eric Schmidt, the billionaire technology executive from Google who became Barack Obama's primary link to Silicon Valley's boardrooms, had played a crucial role in Hillary Clinton's tech election team. 'Key is the development of a single record for a voter that aggregates all that is known about them,' he wrote, in a doubtless unconscious echo of *The Circle*.[4] So why didn't Hillary Clinton win? One among many factors was Cambridge Analytica, which, as Eric Schmidt's company was developing tools for Hillary Clinton, was developing tools for Donald Trump.[5] In May 2017, the *Guardian* published an article 'The great British Brexit robbery: how our democracy was hijacked', revealing that Cambridge Analytica had carried out major digital targeting marketing for Donald Trump's presidential campaign and for then UKIP leader Nigel Farage's Brexit campaign.[6] A year later, it was revealed that Facebook had also played a role in this scandal, and Mark Zuckerberg was called to testify in front of both the American Congress and the European Parliament. Step by step, the big Silicon Valley companies (from Google to Facebook) are shown to be not simply harvesting data but actively interfering in elections.[7] And then, of course, denying any such practice – or, as Mark Zuckerberg did, blaming everything on the Russians.

The dark, prophetic conclusion predicted in *The Circle* is that, instead of influencing governments, Silicon Valley becomes a government on its own.

Yet perhaps this nightmare doesn't lie in the future. Perhaps it's already here. The drones above us can be understood as harbingers of a total digital colonization ('Completion' is Eggers's term) that is already being undertaken by Silicon Valley through the 'internet of things' (a phrase connoting the absolute integration of our homes, vehicles and infrastructure of our lives into one single network); 'smart cities' (the privatization of our cities' infrastructure by Silicon Valley); social networks (Facebook, Twitter, Instagram); Google; transport innovations (drones, Tesla Motors), Big Data, total surveillance, AI, VR and last but not least, 'immortality' (Silicon Valley's dream that we will upload our brains and live for ever). All these fields of massive investment and radical innovation are transforming our reality in such a profound way that every aspect of our lives will soon be integrated into a big global digital Circle.

To appreciate the full implications of what Silicon Valley's great transformation entails, it is useful here to relate it to Italian sociologist and philosopher Maurizio Lazzarato's concept of 'machinic enslavement'.

Based on the French psychotherapist-philosopher Félix Guattari's ideas about 'semio-capitalism' (a capitalism based on the production of signs), machinic enslavement describes how the individual effectively and literally becomes a mere cog in the Machine. In other words, our whole human *process of becoming* or 'subjectivation' goes through the Machine and is entirely dependent on technology. Here, Lazzarato develops his influential concept of 'immaterial labour', a form of labour which incorporates computational control but also human activities that would not previously have been considered as work (language, emotions, desires).[8] If immaterial labour is used to describe cognitive and affective labour that isn't necessarily connected to digital technologies (care labour, consolation, psychological support, communication and even sex), machinic enslavement describes the next stage, in which immaterial labour becomes an integral part of the Machine. Take the call centre, in which communication, words and propositions are the input and output of machinic enslavement specific to service relations. Whereas previously workers used machines which were external to them (tools, factory equipment and so on), now we are all using means which are internal (emotions, language, etc.). This is what French philosopher Bernard Stiegler is talking about in his phrase 'the proletarianization of the human mind' – or more precisely, the extraction of value from the human nervous system.[9]

What we can see here is the way communication becomes part of production. Now, instead of the worker's material output it is their *immateriality* (language, communication, affects) that is being exploited: now, capital profits from the very soul of the worker. This is machinic enslavement. But to really understand the difference between immaterial labour and machinic enslavement we must move from the call centre back to the future, namely, to the dystopian science-fiction reality of the Circle. If in the good old days of the call centre the forms of exploitation were still tangible, in the era of the Circle exploitation becomes invisible. At the 2015 World Economic Forum in Davos, Eric Schmidt himself pronounced that 'the internet will disappear ... you won't even sense it, it will be part of your presence all the time'. What if we just replace the word 'internet' with 'exploitation'; what if you won't even sense how you're being exploited and it becomes a perpetual part of your presence? This is the future we are already living. If in the good old days, especially after the Facebook scandal of 2018, we were still somehow aware that all our 'likes', photos, friendships, emotions and desires were being extracted and sold to so-called 'third parties', the Circle embodies the stage of machinic enslavement in which this immaterial labour becomes an integral part of the Machine (there is no third party, there is only the Silicon Valley party!). The social and emotional core of our being, our friendships and our desires are now not only a cog in the Machine, but are already being pre-programmed and inter-related with other inputs/outputs.

Nowadays machinic enslavement is discernible in China's Social Credit System (a system using Big Data and AI to monitor citizens and score them based on their social, political and economic behaviour). It is present too in the West, where in some countries it is rapidly becoming impossible to use cash (take Sweden, where 80 per cent of all transactions are already digital); where it might become impossible to open the door of your office without an implanted micro-chip (in Sweden, start-ups are offering micro-chips for the working class); or where it might become impossible even to have a date without the Machine checking and setting up your potential partner – or even further, deciding who precisely is your perfect match.

In the fourth season of *Black Mirror* the episode 'Hang the DJ' finally touched on the question of how AI will affect love; it looked like a dystopia from the future only to those who are not yet familiar with the present advances in technology (Tinder, Grindr, 'cyberbutlers', AI choosing our perfect match), which are rapidly turning science fiction into reality. In *Black Mirror*'s future society, romantic encounters are scheduled by the AI system called 'The Coach', which collects data in order to match the user with their 'ultimate compatible other' and dictates which romantic relationship its users will have and for how long.

Let's say you just had a beautiful romantic dinner and the chair is already trembling beneath you because you are falling in love. You go to the toilet and check the Coach in order to see whether this is your perfect match. Unfortunately, the AI says the relationship expires in twelve hours. But don't worry. The more relationships you have, the more data the computer gathers. The more data it gathers, the more accurate it is in personality prediction. It is no coincidence that the model of political message-targeting developed by Cambridge Analytica in order to influence and pre-program elections was based on a 2015 research paper at Cambridge's Psychometrics Centre called 'Computer-based personality judgments are more accurate than those made by humans'.[10] The paper showed how computer models are more accurate in predicting an individual's personality by using Facebook likes than a person's work colleague, cohabitant or friend, family member or spouse. When the computer analysed ten likes, it could predict the personality better than a work colleague; when it analysed seventy, the computer could predict the personality better than a friend or roommate. When it analysed 150 likes, it could predict personality better than a family member and when it analysed 300 (more than the average user of Facebook makes), it could come very close to predicting the personality of the user as well as a spouse or lover. The algorithm knows you better than your friends and almost as well as your spouse.

It is no coincidence that the way Facebook attempted to survive the Cambridge Analytica affair was by immediately announcing the launch of an online dating service called simply 'Dating'. This might sound like a bad joke, but it isn't. Unlike apps such as Tinder or Grindr that use Facebook connections to identify potential matches, Facebook can see almost everything: it can track couples from their first likes to the point at which they're ready for engagement ring ads and beyond. No wonder Bloomberg published an article in May 2018 simply saying 'Facebook is right to think "likes" can lead to love'.[11] Obviously, there is but a small step from pre-programming elections to attempting to pre-program love, and vice versa.

To cut a long story short, the highest stage of machinic enslavement is when you start loving the Machine itself, because the ideology of the transparent society has penetrated so deep that in the end there is no longer any difference between human and machine.

An even darker understanding of our near or already existing future is to be found in Franco 'Bifo' Berardi's book *And: Phenomenology of the End* (2015).

The Italian philosopher, also influenced by Félix Guattari, is one of our most provocative and daring contemporary thinkers, and has been thinking about the impact of technology on human life for over forty years. Bifo argues that a 'mutation' is underway, a mutation that can be neither resisted nor reversed. Through the process of work, he asserts, humans are transformed into 'connected elaborators of information'. To produce and to work implies that we are connected to the Machine: connection equals work. As a consequence, politics also changes. It is time to rethink what politics – and democracy – really means in the early twenty-first century, with Big Tech already influencing and manipulating elections. And more to the point: how much free will (to do anything, including voting) will we really have if our preferences and acts are already predicted and programmed by the algorithm?

What Bifo points out in his 'phenomenology of the end' (technology as the end of politics) is that traditional governments or traditional forms of political order are no longer able to control the flow of information, and that a new 'info-networked super-organism' (like the Circle) is in the process of becoming. And if we are already sucked into a process by which Silicon Valley corporations are replacing governments in the control and processing of taxes, healthcare or education, why, by logical extension, wouldn't they take care of voting? Bifo warns us that this info-networked super-organism is evolving outside the sphere of human decision-making and knowledge; it is becoming automated.

In the last scene of Dave Eggers's novel the inventor and founder of the Circle loses control of his own creature and admits in utter despair:

> I did not intend any of this to happen. And it's moving so fast [. . .] I didn't picture a world where Circle membership was mandatory, where all government and all life was channeled through one network [. . .] There used to be the option of opting out. But now that's over. Completion is the end. We're closing the circle around everyone – it's a totalitarian nightmare.[12]

This, indeed, is the final stage of the ideology of the Transparent Society: the circle of connectivity and transparency, the circle of fake friendships and fake news, the circle of total presence that must become closed. Those who stay outside the circle will become obsolete. Only those who are inside will have a choice. But even this choice will be fake.

Aren't we rapidly approaching such a dystopian world?

If you want to have a job, you have to be connected. If you want to maintain friendships, you have to be connected. If you want to go on a date, you have to be connected. If you want to do anything at all, you have to be in the vicious circle of Facebook, Instagram, Twitter, smart cities, smart everything, emails, apps, etc. If you are out of the circle, it's as if you don't exist. Human interactions themselves have become commodified; every interaction is already a transaction. And there is no transaction without connection.

If before the internet revolution it was a privilege to be connected (such connections applied only to US universities and the military in the beginning; then to the first hackers: only in the mid-1990s did the internet start to become commercialized), today it's a privilege not to be connected. Isn't it remarkable that the Silicon Valley super-rich are increasingly sending their children to elite schools in which iPhones, iPads and even laptops are banned at the same time as they are connecting the majority of the world's population with their tools?[13] Back in 2010, Steve Jobs told the *New York Times* that his children had never used an iPad: 'We limit how much technology our kids use in the home.' 'Never get high on your own supply' is the credo of today's techno-utopian elite. For the rest of us, technology is a drug, an opiate. In December 2017 a former Facebook executive revealed his fears, saying that 'the short-term, dopamine-driven feedback loops that we have created are destroying how society works: no civil discourse, no cooperation, misinformation, mistruth. And it's not an American problem. This is not about Russian ads. This is a global problem.'[14]

Only a month before, early investor in Facebook Sean Parker warned: 'God only knows what it's doing to our children's brains', claiming that the social networks exploit human psychological vulnerabilities through a validation feedback loop that gets people to post constantly in order to get even more likes and comments.[15] Sounds like drugs? Well, that's because it is. More precisely, it should be described as 'Narcocapitalism', 'a capitalism that is narcotic through and through, whose excitability is only the manic reverse of the depression it never stops producing'.[16] This is another good description of the Circle, a never-ending circle of excitation and depression, the impossibility of getting rid of the narcotic rush technology gives us every time we scroll through our social networks or use one of the countless apps supposedly here to make our lives easier and better.

The movie ends. As the credits finish rolling, the screen fades and the night takes its place. I can see the stars above me again. Then, a girl in the audience takes a selfie, with the cinema and stars as the backdrop, and posts the image on Instagram. We obviously already live in the Circle. There is no longer a future, only a constant hyperconnected present.

3
It's the End of the World
(as We Know It . . .)

The present seems to be omnipresent. Yet, no one seems to believe in the future any more. Our world no longer appears connected by a shared hope in a better future; on the contrary, it is hyperconnected by a prevailing feeling that there is no future at all.

What future do the millions of people fleeing wars, poverty or climate change, escaping despair only to find new despair at the borders, camps, central stations and parks of Western cities have? What hope remains when walls are rising from Mexico to Hungary; when new 'smart' borders are being erected and the Schengen agreement (the free movement of persons as a fundamental right guaranteed by the EU to its citizens) is being suspended in the European Union; when terrorist attacks occur in an almost weekly rhythm from London to Istanbul, from Paris to Berlin, from Nice to Munich? Autocratic regimes from Kaczyński's Poland to Orban's Hungary are born as we look on. In front of our eyes, the EU, represented by the Troika (European Commission, European Central Bank, International Monetary Fund), is bringing the countries of Europe's periphery, from Spain to Greece, from Portugal to Croatia, to poverty and despair with more debt and austerity measures. What future – except emigration – do the millions of young people from these countries have? What future, except indefinite debt, do millions of young Europeans have? And what about the rest of the world, from Mexico to India, which is drowning in poverty or violence; what about the vast majority of the world's population who live in despair and without hope? And what if the global poor become victim of an even bigger global catastrophe which will make the current refugee crisis look like a footnote to a much greater humanitarian disaster?

In March 2018, the World Bank published a report containing a projection that by 2050 we can expect 140 million refugees from just three regions – Sub-Saharan Africa, South Asia and South America – as the result of climate change.[1] Why is the World Bank worried about it? Because it will, according to its projections, provoke greater cross-border conflict, rising nationalism, more walls and so on. In other words, the current crisis of Europe – with its authoritarian, xenophobic and militarized regimes, their walls and hatred towards refugees – might pale into insignificance against the dark times ahead. If the current backlash in Europe – a general lurch towards the xenophobic right; barbed-wire fences and detention camps; anti-democratic legislation such as the Hungarian criminalization of migrant helpers[2] – was catalysed by the arrival of around a million migrants and refugees in 2015, what will happen when 140 million look to Europe as their only hope of survival? And what if this is not something that will happen in 2050, but is already tangible now?

Nowadays, it is impossible to avoid imagining the end of our world: we are bombarded with countless daily images and news about our dying planet. Climate change is wiping out ancient baobab trees, while in March 2018 the last northern white male rhino died in Kenya. He was forty-five years old, living under 24/7 armed protection just because his horns and skin are a precious market commodity. Today, we are witnessing the extinction of species that have survived for millions of years, but could not survive us. Meanwhile, Europe's bird population has dropped by more than 400 million in the last thirty years.[3] Why? Because of pesticides there are hardly any insects left for them to eat: flying insects across the continent have declined by 80 per cent. No wonder that around the world, scientists are building repositories of everything from seeds to ice to mammal milk (so-called 'Arks of the Apocalypse'), racing to preserve a natural order that is rapidly disappearing.[4]

This possibility that there is no longer a future isn't only a concern of the scientists or biologists. It has become the prevailing feeling, the prevailing reality of the global poor. It is now the anxious dinner-table talk of a middle class that is losing ground across the globe. It has spread west and south, north and east, to all corners of the Earth. Finally, it has reached the global rich. On 30 January 2017, the *New*

Yorker published an article entitled 'Doomsday prep for the super-rich'.[5] The rich are not unaware of the possibility of global catastrophe; they're expecting it and preparing for it.

The CEO of Reddit, Steve Huffman, explains he underwent corrective laser eye surgery because getting contacts or glasses 'is going to be a huge pain in the ass' in the event of a global disaster. As Evan Osnos describes in the *New Yorker*, 'he is less focused on a specific threat' – a quake on the San Andreas fault, a pandemic, a dirty bomb – than he is on the aftermath or, as he puts it, 'the temporary collapse of our government and structures'. 'I own a couple of motorcycles. I have a bunch of guns and ammo. Food. I figure that, with that, I can hole up in my house for some amount of time.'[6]

Another Silicon Valley denizen, Antonio García Martínez, author of *Chaos Monkeys*, a book comparing Silicon Valley to the 'chaos monkeys' of society, bought five wooded acres on an island in the Pacific Northwest and equipped it with generators, solar panels and thousands of rounds of ammunition. As the *New Yorker* vividly describes, 'On private Facebook groups, wealthy survivalists swap tips on gas masks, bunkers and locations safe from the effects of climate change.'

It comes as no surprise that the PayPal co-founder and Facebook board member Peter Thiel, once Donald Trump's closest tech-adviser, became an honorary Kiwi, joining a growing band of wealthy Americans – and they are mainly from Silicon Valley – seeking safe haven in New Zealand from a possible global catastrophe. Some have speculated that doomsday fears are fuelling the country's interest rates. Reid Hoffman, a co-founder of LinkedIn and a prominent investor, admitted to the *New Yorker* that, among the wealthy, interest in the island is code for having a plan B in case of civilization's collapse. 'Saying you're "buying a house in New Zealand" is kind of a wink, wink, say no more. Once you've done the Masonic handshake, they'll be, like, "Oh, you know, I have a broker who sells old ICBM silos, and they're nuclear-hardened, and they kind of look like they would be interesting to live in." '

Another article vividly embodying the current apocalyptic *zeitgeist* was published in June 2017 by *Forbes* under the title 'The shocking doomsday maps of the world and the billionaire escape plans'.[7] The piece set forth a futuristic vision of Earth ravaged by flooding or hit by an asteroid which could cause the entire planet to shift its axis of rotation, and offered an overview of the real-existing escape plans: namely, how the richest families have been grabbing up massive amounts of farmland around the world. All such property is far away from coastal areas, in locations propitious for self-survival, farming and coal mining. Dry territories in the United States such as Montana, New Mexico, Wyoming and Texas are very popular regions for the wealthiest billionaires, such as John Malone (former CEO of Tele-Communications Inc. and the largest landowner in America), who owns 2,200,000 acres including areas in Wyoming and Colorado; Ted Turner (2,000,000 acres in Montana, Nebraska, New Mexico and North Dakota); Philip Anschultz (434,000 acres in Wyoming); Amazon's Jeff Bezos (400,000 acres in Texas) and Stan Kroenke (225,162 acres in Montana). Many billionaires are preparing for future escape with vacation homes, silos and bunkers in remote locations. Many of them also have private planes ready to depart at a moment's notice.[8]

According to *Forbes*, moguls in Australia and New Zealand have been snapping up farmland at record pace as well. 'The interest in cattle, dairy and agricultural farms are all proving tempting for self-sustained survival,' but 'more importantly the wealthy are preparing for safe escape havens, stockpiling real estate in dry areas and moving away from the old-school approach of storing food and water. Money and precious metals will be useless, as self-sustainable territory will become the new necessary luxury.'[9]

Besides giving an overview of the already existing escape plans, *Forbes* published a detailed list of predicted land changes predicated on geological positioning based on futurologist theories (from Gordon-Michael Scallion to Edgar Cayce). The whole world will come to resemble the post-apocalyptic science-fiction film *Waterworld*, in which Kevin Costner plays one of the rare survivors who sails the Earth in his trimaran after the sea levels have risen due to global warming, wiping out entire regions. But unlike the *Waterworld* scenario, today's billionaires don't intend to sail off in search of Dryland. Way back in 2008 Peter Thiel launched a mission to develop a floating libertarian utopia in the middle of the ocean, called 'Seasted', that would serve as a permanent, politically autonomous settlement in the event that the sea level rises due to global warming. So even if the rest of the world goes to hell, there might still be some surviving libertarian utopias.

Since that time, the spectre of the coming apocalypse has been edging deeper into mainstream culture. In 2012, the National Geographic Channel launched *Doomsday Preppers*, a reality show featuring a series of Americans bracing themselves for what they called S.H.T.F. (shit hits the fan). The première drew more than 4 million viewers, and by the end of the first season it was the most popular show in the channel's history. A survey commissioned by *National Geographic* found that 40 per cent of Americans believed that stocking up on supplies or building a bomb shelter was a wiser investment than a 401(k), a retirement savings plan in the United States.

This sense of the impending collapse of civilization has penetrated deep into the popular imagination: not as a distant possibility but as the darkest of all possible futures lurking on the horizon.

All of which brings us to the election of Donald Trump as the forty-fifth president of the United States and his contribution to the apocalyptic *zeitgeist*. In his inaugural address on 20 January 2017, the new president outlined the collapse of civilization:

> But for too many of our citizens, a different reality exists: Mothers and children trapped in poverty in our inner cities; rusted-out factories scattered like tombstones across the landscape of our nation; an education system, flush with cash, but which leaves our young and beautiful students deprived of knowledge; and the crime and gangs and drugs that have stolen too many lives and robbed our country of so much unrealized potential.[10]

In this address, far from admitting that he himself might be the reason for the apocalyptic fears and disasters to come, Donald Trump has left his critics far behind, sprawled in the dust. He outlines a phantasmagoric landscape, in which he appears as the Saviour. At the end of his speech, he declaimed that 'We stand at the birth of a new millennium.' Although the new millennium had, at least according to the calendar, started seventeen years previously, in Trump's mind the new millennium could now start – now that he had arrived.

This was no slip of the tongue; it was more a sleight of hand. Trump, or some of his key advisers, knew perfectly well that 'millennium' refers to the 'end of times' and the Second Coming, which is exactly the reason why he used such language. In the Book of Revelation, a.k.a. the 'Apocalypse of John', the close of the millennium and Christ's Second Coming are figured forth:

> Then I saw a new heaven and a new earth, for the first heaven and the
> first earth had passed away, and there was no longer any sea. I saw the
> Holy City, the new Jerusalem, coming down out of heaven from God,
> prepared as a bride beautifully dressed for her husband. And I heard a
> loud voice from the throne saying, 'Now the dwelling of God is with
> men, and He will live with them. They will be His people, and God
> Himself will be with them and be their God.' (Revelation 21:1–3, NIV)

For Christ, read Trump. As in the Second Coming, when the wicked are overwhelmed with terror and despair, Trump's speech depicted a pre-apocalyptic situation in which everyone was waiting for the Messiah. Instead of the 'Apocalypse of John', we obviously have the 'Apocalypse of Donald'. The ancient Greek *apokalyptein* ('apocalypse') signifies 'disclosure' or 'revelation'. Here, then, was Donald Trump's 'revelation'.

No wonder the Vatican, only a few months after Donald Trump's first visit to Pope Francis in May 2017, accused the White House of 'apocalyptic geopolitics'. In a piece published in the Catholic journal *La Civiltà Cattolica* on 13 July 2017 – days after US evangelical leaders met Donald Trump in the Oval Office of the White House and 'laid hands'[11] on him in prayer following discussions about religious freedom, support for Israel and healthcare reform – two close associates of Pope Francis accused the United States of 'evangelical fundamentalism', by which they meant that he had adopted a twisted reading of scripture on issues ranging from climate change to migration.

The reason the Vatican doesn't like Trump is that his administration uses fake religious arguments to demonize segments of the population – particularly migrants and Muslims, women and the alt-left – and to promote the United States as a nation that is blessed by

God, without ever taking into account the 'bond between capital and profits and arms sales'.[12]

'In this Manichaean vision,' claim the two close associates of Pope Francis, 'belligerence can acquire a theological justification and there are pastors who seek a biblical foundation for it, using scriptural texts out of context.'

Trump's inauguration speech was the launchpad for this 'apocalyptic narrative'. 'In this theological vision,' the papal authors assert, 'natural disasters, dramatic climate change and the global ecological crisis are not only not perceived as an alarm that should lead them to reconsider their dogmas, but they are seen as the complete opposite: signs that confirm their non-allegorical understanding of the final figures of the Book of Revelation and their apocalyptic hope in a "new heaven and a new earth".'

This was perhaps Trump's biggest con, to use New Testament texts about the conquest and defence of the 'promised land' (here, the United States), and present himself as his own 'revelation', a sort of postmodern messiah who has arrived to save us from the prevailing decadence and decay described in the inaugural 'Apocalypse of Donald'.

Looking back on it now, the birth of the apocalyptic narrative, from Trump's inauguration speech to the grim scenarios conjured up by the leading global media, might just about be the biggest discursive shift of our times. Discourse always has real consequences. In the forty-eight hours after Trump was elected, according to the *Guardian*'s article 'Silicon Valley super-rich head south to escape from a global apocalypse', New Zealand government immigration websites saw a 2,500 per cent increase in traffic.[13] Immigration New Zealand received 88,353 visits from the US, up from 2,300 visits a day. The investor-focused New Zealand Now website received 101,000 visits from the US in the same two-day period, compared with its usual daily average of 1,500.

If, before 2017, we were all living in what in psychoanalytical terms could be described as 'fetishist denial', then from Trump's election onwards we are living in something that could best be described as 'apocalyptic fetishism'.

The notion of fetishist denial was coined by the French psychoanalyst Octave Mannoni in his famous essay '*Je sais bien, mais quand même*'

('I know perfectly well, but . . .') where he puts forward a theory all too apposite to our current apocalyptic *zeitgeist*.[14] According to Mannoni, in fetishist denial the subject is able at the same time to believe in his fantasy and to recognize that it is nothing but a fantasy. If Marx's definition of ideology was 'they do not know what they're doing but they do it', fetishist denial might be described as 'they know what they're doing and they're still doing it'.[15] The problem, from the viewpoint of psychoanalysis, is of course that the individual's acknowledgement of the fantasy in no way reduces the power that fantasy has over the individual.

Before Trump, faced with the prospect of terrible natural disasters and radical climate change, nuclear wars and even our planet's destruction, we would usually answer this fear with '*Je sais bien, mais quand même*'. In other words, it was as though the majority of the world's population was suffering from a global fetishist denial: we knew it but we were still doing it. 'We know very well that we might be living in the end of times, that a natural disaster could wipe out whole countries or that a nuclear war might wipe out the whole planet, but . . .' Then follows a variety of denials: 'the world is always on the brink of destruction, yet it continues to survive; there's no such thing as climate change; there's nothing we can do about it anyhow', etc.

As if out of the blue (as if, that is, decades of scientific research, indicating overwhelmingly that human-made climate change is a fact, didn't mean anything), summer 2017 arrived. The world was hit by once-in-1,000-years storms and powerful hurricanes (Harvey, Irma, Maria and Nate) and ecological disasters (from Greenland to California), as if giving material shape to the worst apocalyptic fears of recent years. Then came summer 2018, with lethal wildfires in Greece and record heatwaves and droughts across Europe (from London to Berlin), prompting CNN to claim 'Deadly heat waves have become more common due to climate change',[16] while the *Guardian* predicted that 'Unsurvivable heatwaves could strike heart of China by end of century'.[17] Here was, once again, the perfect moment for a collective awakening from the global slumber of fetishist denial. What happened instead is something that can be best described as 'fetishist apocalypticism'.

What we can see in these visions of the future and Donald Trump's apocalyptic geopolitics is an evolution of fetishist denialism. No longer is it a case of 'we know the end of the world is nigh, and do nothing'. Now it's a case of knowing the end of the world is nigh – so, we prepare for it.

And it is not so difficult to reveal the real ideological core behind this fetishist apocalypticism. The main question seems to be not so much what will happen to the global poor if climate change leads to a post-apocalyptic *Waterworld* or *The Day After Tomorrow*, but how the rich will be able to escape. There's no public interest here, only private. Fetishist apocalypticism doesn't bother to ask what we can change now in order to avoid the apocalypse. Rather, it's how can we – or, more precisely, the mega-rich – survive the apocalypse when it happens?

On the one hand, we have the majority of the world's population either in denial or watching helplessly what is happening; on the other, we have the global mega-rich, themselves largely responsible for the coming apocalypse (wars, global warming, etc.), but already working on personal escape plans, from bunkers and sea cities to the colonization of Mars. Nowhere was this so tangible as in the case of the wildfires that devastated California in late 2018; while the rich residents of Malibu were rescued by yachts, many of the poor in Paradise were unsuccessfully trying to flee on foot.

At first glance, we might naively conclude that fetishist denialism and fetishist apocalypticism stand in opposition to each other. One describes a helpless passivity (nothing can be changed anyhow); the other suggests an agency, a readiness to act, to be prepared for that which can't be changed anyhow. But in fact, both responses rest on the idea that there's nothing that can be done to avoid the apocalypse.

What is missing is a real alternative to both these fetishisms: a third option that goes beyond both. But if this third answer is neither to deny the apocalypse nor to prepare for it, what is it?

In order to get outside the current deadlock of what the British cultural theorist Mark Fisher once described as 'the slow cancellation of the future',[18] we need what the French engineer and philosopher Jean-Pierre Dupuy, best known for his work on catastrophism, calls 'enlightened doom-saying'. What Dupuy argues is that what might seem impossible – a global-scale ecological catastrophe, for instance, or an Armageddon-inducing nuclear war – is nonetheless, based on our present knowledge, inevitable. Assuming that one of these catastrophes is our destiny, there is something we can do. We can retroactively change the conditions of possibility out of which this destiny will come.

To understand what this sort of enlightened doom-saying might mean, it's worth taking a look at Denis Villeneuve's recent science-fiction film *Arrival* (2016), which deals with the sudden and unexpected arrival of aliens on Earth. Predictably, humans, unable to understand something so completely beyond their imagining, sink into chaos, from fundamentalist suicide groups to world powers leading the planet into a final, global war. After all else fails, a linguist is asked to join the US team of scientists to find out why the aliens came to Earth in the first place. Once she's learnt their language, the linguist is able to ask what the aliens want. They answer: 'Offer weapon.' At the same time, similar but different translations ('use weapon') are inferred in other parts of the world, leading China to interpret the alien response as a threat. With Earth on the verge of suicidal annihilation, the linguist has a moment of epiphany, realizing that what humans interpreted as 'weapon' might have an alternative translation such as 'tool': slowly, following the Sapir–Whorf linguistic hypothesis that language determines thought, she understands that this tool is Time. So thanks to a dream-vision she succeeds in getting hold of the private phone number of the Chinese general, calls him and saves the planet.

In *Arrival*, instead of the present leading towards the future, it is the other way round: the future acts upon the present, thus changing the coordinates of what is possible, creating the potential for different outcomes of a situation that seemed determined.

Another term for this inversion of future and present, this kind of enlightened doom-saying – which unlike our two fetishes discussed earlier has an emancipatory potential, able to free us from otherwise unavoidable future catastrophe – would be what the German philosopher Frank Ruda calls 'fatalism'. Ruda's work aims to abolish freedom and re-establish fatalism, but not in a deterministic sense: rather in a dialectical transformation of fatalism into the precondition of freedom itself . This fatalism involves trying to imagine 'the very comet that may devastate the earth, not by imagining it as coming from outer space

POETRY FROM THE FUTURE

some time in the future', but as an event that, 'although unacknowledged, has already occurred'. Through such an inversion we may be able, according to Ruda, to imagine another form of freedom.

In other words, as the Sex Pistols famously said in the 1970s, there is 'No future'. Yet it is precisely this slow cancellation of the future that carries the potential for the creation of an alternative, genuine future: something entirely distinct from this permanent decay, this continuous state of exception and slow suicide of human civilization. If the apocalypse is already occurring (in the sense that a future global-scale catastrophe, based on our present knowledge, is indeed inevitable), then there is a chance of creating a better future out of these post-apocalyptic ruins and once the dust has settled after the collapse of civilization. If it's the end of the world (as we know it . . .), then it is about time to create a new one.

4

The Leftovers in Europe

If ever there was a contemporary cultural product that embodies all facets and contradictions of our current apocalyptic *zeitgeist*, then it is without doubt the recent HBO series *Leftovers*. The series opens three years after a global event called the 'Sudden Departure': the unexplained disappearance of 2 per cent of the world's population (around 140 million people), on 14 October 2011.

In the first season we follow the daily reality of the fictional town of Mapleton, New York, and its inhabitants. Almost everyone in the town has lost someone and is struggling with immense grief. A mother is sitting in her car talking on the phone when all of a sudden her child disappears from the back seat. Another woman, Nora, is at home while her two children and husband are having lunch and suddenly vanish. But life, despite its traumas, slowly starts returning to some form of normality. However, the 'return of the repressed' (the process whereby repressed elements preserved in the unconscious tend to reappear) is lurking behind this seemingly functioning reality.

Some, not wanting to continue as if nothing had happened, join a quasi-religious community called the 'Guilty Remnant': a nihilist group dressed in white monks' habits, who don't speak and endlessly smoke cigarettes (as a declaration of their faith and conviction that there's no future). They stalk another group who wish to find out why the 'Sudden Departure' happened, and in the end they turn into a sort of terrorist group. The Guilty Remnant are the 'Living Reminders' of what happened. For them there can be no meaning. Struggling with meaning belongs to the Old World: it is pointless. What the first season of *Leftovers* shows us are the various ways in which humans react to an inexplicable traumatic event: from denial to nihilism, from mourning to melancholy.

In the second season, the lead characters relocate to the fictional town of Jarden, in the fictional National Park called 'Miracle'. Miracle has become a place of pilgrimage, a heavily guarded gated community for the lucky 9,261 citizens, none of whom went missing in the Sudden Departure. New inhabitants are permitted to move there only in exceptional cases. Yet this place soon proves a false Eden, a paradise that was lost long ago. As the new inhabitants come to realize, it now more than anything else resembles a state of exception.

The third and final season unfolds three years later. Between the closing of the second series and the start of the third, the world has gone mad. It opens fourteen days before the enigmatic seventh anniversary of the Sudden Departure, with events taking the main characters to Australia. In the first episode a French submarine officer launches a nuclear missile at an uninhabited island in the South Pacific in the belief that he's targeting the egg of a monster inside an underwater volcano, which is supposed to hatch seven years after the Sudden Departure and wipe out humanity.

At the same time, across the world in Australia, a group has rented a ferry for an orgy in celebration of an elderly lion named Fraiser, who sired thirty-five cubs before he died. (Here again we can see different reactions to the Sudden Departure played out: fetishist denial to apocalyptic fetishism and all the variations in between.)

In the final episode, one of the main characters, Nora, succeeds in crossing to the other side of her world, where her children and husband have been spirited away. It is at the series' end that things become particularly interesting (spoiler alert). We realize that the departed didn't end up in Eden or a sort of post-human paradise. Rather, they still live in a different, parallel reality. As Nora says upon her return, 'Over here, we lost some of them. But over there, they lost all of us.'

In the final twist of the series, we realize that at the same time as the majority of the world population is struggling to come to terms with their loss, a minority (2 per cent) is living in an even worse reality. Instead of being two different worlds, both realities are intrinsically linked to each other: two sides of one miserable, mad world.

Like *The Man in the High Castle*, the series based on Philip K. Dick's novel, *Leftovers* explores the possibility of parallel realities which are not just alternative scenarios of the same world but which exist simultaneously: different potentialities realized at the same time. The world of the majority and the world of the minority are in fact *the very same world*, the point being that one can't see the other.

As well as being a psychological exploration of our reactions to an inexplicable event, *Leftovers* poses an important political question for our current *zeitgeist*: what if the apocalypse isn't something to come, but is already here? What if your point of view depends just on which side you are, on the reality you had the luck to inhabit?

If the ongoing refugee crisis, which impacted on Europe's consciousness back in 2015, has shown anything – anything, that is, besides the broadly cynical reaction of Western Europe in the face of an exceptionally severe humanitarian disaster – it is this short circuit between two parallel realities: the Western one, which for decades existed in a kind of protected Miracle dwelling between denialism and nihilism; and the reality of the rest of humanity struggling to survive.

The analogy goes further. When the rest of humanity – refugees who are the product of our own military interventions in Africa and the Middle East – started to penetrate the Miracle, the privileged minority reacted with walls, electrified fences and militarization. For the first time after the 'End of History' (the American political scientist Francis Fukuyama's notion that with the fall of the Berlin Wall liberal democracy became the only player in town), it is as if the West was confronted with the coming apocalypse. Yet the apocalypse was already present: it simply hadn't yet reached our little protected enclave of reality.

Suddenly, reality intruded into our Miracle: millions of refugees trying to reach this apparent safe zone, from war-torn countries such as Libya, Syria, Afghanistan, Iraq, Niger or Congo; at the same time, inside our borders terrorist attacks started occurring in a regular rhythm across Europe: from Paris to Brussels, from Munich to Nice, from London to Istanbul. The methods of terror are many and various: ploughing into crowds in trucks and vans (London, Nice), slaughtering with machetes (London, Paris), suicide bombs (Manchester), mowing down with guns at concerts (Paris) and shopping centres (Munich) are no longer an exception but the rule. Europe's response has been draconian: the suspension of free movement between countries as enshrined in the Schengen agreement; the building of electrified fences and watch towers; drones, heat sensors and 'border hunters' (teams of volunteer recruits); the guarding of potential targets – major European airports, shopping centres and metros – not by the police, but by special forces or the army.

In our response to such terrorist atrocities, we always have to bear in mind the lesson of *Leftovers*: there are two realities always co-existing, always present.

Visiting Brussels just after the 2015 terrorist attack, I took a taxi from the airport to the city centre. With typical liberal Eurocentrism, I complained to my black taxi driver how terrible it is that our cities are now turned into war zones, with heavily armed soldiers at the airport and armed vehicles on the streets. To which he calmly replied: 'I come from Congo, for us this is normal.' Realizing that it was another 'short circuit', I responded naively: 'Yes, but in Europe it wasn't normal.' While they have been living in the reality of colonialism for centuries (remember that, during King Leopold II's reign, 10 million Congolese were killed in what was then the Belgian Congo), and are currently (due to the pillage by big Western companies of resources used to produce our smart phones) living through a brutal civil war, the presence of the army and armed police on European streets has only recently become something normal.

If we're going to avoid this Eurocentric liberal trap, our thinking has to evolve. We have to ask why all this – the refugee crisis, terrorism, the militarization of our cities – wasn't normal in Europe until this point. Or, to put it another way, why was it normal in all other parts of the world, but not in the West?

To answer this, we must first dismantle the ideological narrative which has been adopted by governments and mainstream media, even human rights organizations, in the years since the flows of refugees to Europe started in earnest. Indeed, the use of seemingly neutral words such as 'flows' and 'started' reveals the ideological foundation of the 2015 refugee crisis. Refugees were invariably depicted as arriving in 'waves' or 'floods', which were 'streaming' or 'flowing' into Europe. The then British prime minister David Cameron went so far as to describe them as a 'swarm'.[1] Such terms, even if innocently deployed, added up to a picture of the crisis as some kind of natural disaster: all of a sudden, out of the blue, waves of immigrants were flooding into the heart of Europe.

This is exactly how ideology functions. Ideology invariably relies on incorporating events into a discourse that appears natural. If there is one lesson to take away from the French philosopher Roland Barthes's teaching on ideology, it is his far-reaching insight that ideology functions by transforming history (a process which is at the same time political and social) into 'nature'.[2] Using this framework, we can say emphatically that the refugee crisis was not, is not, a natural disaster. It has concrete historical and political roots. All of which allows us to correct a number of misconceptions.

First of all, the refugee crisis did not start in 2015. What countries such as Germany, Austria, Hungary, France, Serbia, Croatia, Slovenia, etc. experienced that year was something that territories on Europe's periphery – Greece, Macedonia, southern Italy, especially Lampedusa – have been experiencing for years. The decisive reason why the refugee crisis was in the spotlight in 2015 lies in one banal but brutal fact: its penetration from the continent's edge to the heart of the European Union.

What we can see here is a short circuit between two parallel realities. During the last two decades the countries of the EU's core – Germany, Austria, France – have lived in placid tranquillity while the EU's periphery experienced a different reality. From time to time, short circuits would, of course, manifest themselves: the 2005 protests in the French *banlieues* and in Denmark a year later. Meanwhile, the 2005 confrontation between Nicolas Sarkozy, then France's minister of the interior, and the angry and desperate immigrants proved the perfect embodiment of the conflict and the political and humanitarian disaster to come.

As the Paris *banlieues* burned, Sarkozy declared a zero tolerance policy towards immigrants, and called them *racaille* ('scum' or 'rabble').[3] Years later, as president, Sarkozy – who, like Cameron, referred to refugees as a 'swarm' – pushed for the British and French-led NATO bombing of Libya which, in 2011, led to the end of Muammar Gaddafi's regime.

As a direct result of Gaddafi's downfall, Islamic State gained a foothold in Libya. A year later, then US president Barack Obama openly criticized Sarkozy and Cameron for the Libya 'mess', saying that it was largely the failure of France and the UK to 'follow up' on their bombing campaign that had led to the current situation.[4] What Obama didn't tackle was the question of why this 'shit show', as he described it, happened in the first place. His problem was the follow up, not the bombing itself.

If we want to get to the root cause of the increasing number of terrorist attacks in Europe in recent years, we have to go back to the 2011 intervention in Libya, which led to a brutal civil war with rival militias vying for power. What is prevailingly presented as a natural disaster is the result of deliberate European foreign policy, backed by the United States, that led to brutal military interventions in Libya, Afghanistan, Syria and Iraq that devastated countries, forcing their populations to flee and brought about the spread of ISIS terrorism. No wonder that of the 25.4 million refugees worldwide, 6.3 million are from Syria and 2.6 million from Afghanistan. It is sufficient to remember the role of the West to understand why this 'boomerang' is now coming back. It's anything but a natural catastrophe.

Ideology can be found at work too in the discourse about immigrants, especially the never-ending semantic battle around the difference between 'economic migrants' and 'refugees'.

Although there is a difference between those fleeing war and migrants searching for better (or indeed any) jobs, we have to understand that poverty ('searching for better jobs') is the result of a structural problem. Nowadays, when it seems that only Syrian refugees are given the right to be defined as such, we are once again turning a blind eye to all the other ongoing conflicts, from Afghanistan to Iraq, from Niger to Mali, from Sudan to Somalia. People fleeing these countries are now immediately lumped together as economic migrants. But the poverty and misery existing in Afghanistan or Iraq are also a consequence of war and brutal economic logic, of what the sociologist Saskia Sassen would call 'expulsions' and the Marxist geographer David Harvey 'accumulation by dispossession'.[5]

In times of economic warfare what is an economic migrant but a refugee? And vice versa. Every refugee is already an economic migrant, because the refugee crisis is a product of the global capitalist economy. It can be traced back to the centuries of colonialism which plunged many Global South countries into an abyss of under-development and reliance on the West (financial institutions such as the IMF or big transnational corporations), which in return did everything – including backing brutal dictators – to keep them underdeveloped in order to harness their cheap labour or exploit their precious natural resources. Military interventions and wars in the twentieth century, in those countries which already suffered from colonialism, didn't make the situation any better. Now, the peoples of many African, Latin American or Middle Eastern countries have no other option but to flee to the West.

In May 2016, working on a documentary film on Europe's refugee emergency for Al Jazeera, I went to visit the northern Greek village of Idomeni, close to the Macedonian border.[6] Idomeni was the informal crossing point through which hundreds of thousands of refugees entered Macedonia in 2015. They started camping there when the Macedonian government began shutting down the border. In November that year the site became a full-scale camp and an emblem of Europe's failure to manage the refugee crisis. Here was a humanitarian disaster: one inevitably portrayed by the media in terms of 'floods' and 'waves', with the refugees regarded as a tide of dangerous intruders who threatened to engulf Europe. When the 'Balkan Route' was closed in March 2016 with the entry into force of the EU–Turkey deal, just two months before we got to Idomeni, these refugees were dispersed into different camps all over Greece, where they live in a kind of humanitarian and legal limbo. Unable to return to their own countries, unable to move forward, they are, in the French philosopher Roland Barthes's prescient phrase, the 'integrated reject'.[7]

At one of the camps near Thessaloniki, I had the opportunity to meet Mustafa Alhamoud. He is from Aleppo, twenty-four years old, and fled together with his family hoping to reach Western Europe. Not for economic reasons, but to save his family's life. What happened when he finally reached Idomeni? Europe closed its borders, Austria sent its troops to the Macedonian frontier, and they were trapped, together with 12,000 other people.

Fed up with the mainstream media's portrayal of refugees as 'dangerous intruders' or a 'natural disaster', Mustafa and his Syrian friends created Refugee TV. It began as a parody with a fake camera made out of wood and a plastic bottle (something like Michel Gondry's comedy film *Be Kind Rewind*, only much darker). Soon, though, it became a real online news outlet giving a voice to those otherwise voiceless and telling the real and courageous stories of ordinary people fleeing a brutal war.

Mustafa's own story is a case in point. He and his family fled Syria, through Turkey, and by boat to Greece. They spent a freezing winter in Idomeni, hoping the borders to Northern Europe would open again. Now, together with around a thousand other refugees, they live at the Oreokastro camp, a gigantic old military hangar surrounded by the Greek army, with hundreds of tents pitched in it. Mustafa shows us round the camp, though he is sick with a fever of 40°C. There are toilets and showers, but nothing else – not even hope. For Mustafa, Idomeni was relatively free and open: they at least had a hope of crossing the border and reaching Western Europe. Here, nothing.

We leave and make our way to Idomeni itself. It takes around an hour by car. It is not yet summer, but in Greece it already feels like it. We drive away from Thessaloniki, where tourists are beginning to colonize the beaches, towards the Greek–Macedonian border. The closer we get, the more surreal the scene. A motorway service station is transformed into a temporary shelter by those refusing the government camps: hundreds of refugees, including the elderly and children. The service station allows them to stay – and is doing good business charging them for showers.

After passing several checkpoints, we approach Idomeni. Suddenly, the countryside is quiet. The silence is expectant; there's a feeling of having entered an area that's off limits. Mustafa guides us round the deserted town, showing us where the refugees' tents were pitched. 'Now it's 100 per cent changed, I feel like it's not the same place,' he says. We reach the railway station, where barely two months before 12,000 people were camping. There, Mustafa explains that the refugees, encamped on the train tracks, were engaged in an act of non-violent resistance: preventing the movement of goods from the Aegean Sea (the now Chinese-owned Port of Piraeus) to the heart of Europe. In doing so, they hoped Europe might finally listen to them.

Back in 1964 the American activist Mario Savio, a key member of the Berkeley Free Speech Movement – which, inspired by the struggle for civil rights, was to drive opposition to the Vietnam War – declared that

> There's a time when the operation of the machine becomes so odious, makes you so sick at heart, that you can't take part! You can't even passively take part! And you've got to put your bodies upon the gears and upon the wheels . . . upon the levers, upon all the apparatus, and you've got to make it stop! And you've got to indicate to the people who run it, to the people who own it, that unless you're free, the machine will be prevented from working at all![8]

Some sixty years later, Savio's words apply perfectly to the situation Mustafa and his fellow refugees found themselves in. Sitting at the rail tracks where only a few months earlier he and 12,000 other refugees had put their bodies 'upon the gears' and 'upon the levers', Mustafa gestures towards the peaceful countryside around Idomeni, and says: 'If we had occupied the nearby fields, nothing would have happened. By occupying the train tracks every day we were at least visible!' Later, an official of the Hellenic Train Organization admitted to me that they had to solve the 'refugee problem' because they were unable to run trains on this stretch of track for seventy-five days, costing them $2.5 million in lost shipping fees.[9]

A week later, I made my way across Europe to the northeastern French border, to Western Europe's counterpart to Idomeni. The camp at Calais hadn't been cleared yet. I talked to a representative of Eurostar, the company responsible for operating the Eurotunnel between France and Britain, and whose turnover is some $100 billion a year. They were keen to get rid of the Calais camp for the very same reason that Greece wanted to disperse the camp at Idomeni. Because the refugees who wanted to board the trains and reach Britain had become a problem for the free circulation of capital.[10]

Soon after my visit, the Calais camp was demolished and its inhabitants forcibly displaced. Today, Calais has the most sophisticated surveillance system I've ever seen, with drones surveilling the perimeter fencing. The Eurostar official I met had proudly drawn my attention to the 2-metre high-tech fences behind us. These, he declared, were NATO-standard fences, the same kind used to protect the elites during international summits. The same fences used to defend the G20 from the 'rabble' in Hamburg in July 2017.

There is, of course, another twist to the story. Those refugees lucky enough to have reached and found a place in the Miracle came to realize that the European Union was in reality a paradise that was long ago lost – if indeed it had ever existed. Instead of offering solidarity, jobs and peace, this place called 'Europe' is now in a permanent state of exception. There is no escape. Except, maybe, for the very rich.

A perfect manifestation of this is what in Sweden is termed the *Uppgivenhetssyndrom*, or 'resignation syndrome'. A recent phenomenon, this condition started to manifest itself among refugee children – mainly from former Soviet and Yugoslav states – arriving in Sweden. After undertaking tortuous, traumatic journeys to Europe, only to wait in vain for asylum once there, refugee children were, according to the medical journal *Acta Paediatrica*, rendered 'totally passive, immobile, lacks tonus, withdrawn, mute, unable to eat and drink, incontinent and not reacting to physical stimuli or pain'.[11]

Although the *Uppgivenhetssyndrom* is said to exist only in Sweden, and only among refugees, isn't this resignation syndrome, the incapability, literally, to get out of bed or to leave one's room – and, metaphorically, in the sense of giving up, losing all hope – something that is increasingly characteristic of our times?

5

Make Margaret Atwood
Fiction Again!

Every day, since the time we learned how to walk, we take thousands of steps. We take steps with our fathers and mothers, our friends and lovers; we climb hills and furniture; we go to our jobs or islands. Those of us who are already part of the Circle use tracking apps which count our steps, record the distance we've covered, the time we're active, our heart rate and calories burned.

How surprised we would be if, instead of measuring our steps in the manner of data that needs to be crunched (the essence of capitalism, of course, which now commodifies even the paces we take), there existed a mechanism that enabled us to become truly aware of the potential possibilities inherent in the steps we take: steps which might lead us into the worst of all possible futures.

You can find *Stolpersteine* (literally, 'stumbling stones') in most major European cities. Every one of these is a portal into a really existing world: small, 10 x 10-centimetre, concrete cubes, each of which bears a plate inscribed with the names and life dates of victims of Nazi extermination or persecution. As of January 2017, over 56,000 *Stolpersteine* have been laid in twenty-two European countries, making them the world's largest decentralized memorial.

In Nazi Germany there was an antisemitic saying, when someone accidentally stumbled over a protruding stone: 'A Jew must be buried here.' The *Stolpersteine* gave material form to this saying, and in so doing turned it against itself. Yes, the stones say, Jews – and others – are buried below our steps. The stones make us aware.

Here the Latin *calculus* ('a pebble or stone used for counting') acquires the literal meaning of a stone used for counting the victims of the Holocaust. But there's more to the *Stolpersteine* than a powerful reminder. These stumbling stones, especially when you literally trip over them in places in Kreuzberg or Cologne, are also a measure of the potentialities of our own steps. In these stones, our steps cross paths with those of others, those whose steps led towards the concentration camps.

Typically, the *Stolpersteine* are placed in front of houses and places from which people were taken away to the camps. The immediate effect, therefore, is completely different from that of a visit to some of the preserved concentration camps, such as Auschwitz or Lublin.

A visit to one of these camps makes one aware of a new resonance to 'concentrated': it is overwhelming, beyond language. With the *Stolpersteine*, however, meaning becomes inscribed in your own steps. The stones present a deep intrusion into our everyday life: living reminders that, unlike those who suddenly disappear, we are, truly, the 'Leftovers', the ones who stayed alive.

The suffering of the millions who died in concentration camps is numinous, too much to comprehend. Yet the simple words written on most of the stumbling stones, *Hier wohnte . . .* ('Here lived . . .'), emphasize that the victims of persecution did not live and work in some abstract place: they were right here, they were us.

It is from right here that someone's steps led to the concentration camps. With the stones, the stories of Holocaust victims are no longer abstractions, difficult to discern. The individual fates of all the Jews, Sinti and Romani, African-Caribbeans, gays, communists and anti-Nazi resistance fighters, the physically or mentally disabled, are now given particular, distinct clarity. Their steps vanished precisely where our steps walk on, into the still open future.

Imagine that we had such *Stolpersteine* to enable us to trace current horrors. Imagine if we could walk in the steps of the millions of refugees and displaced people throughout Europe or of those tens of millions entrapped in the camps of Lebanon, Libya and elsewhere – but did so before it is again too late. If we stumbled upon the stones of other people's fates and saw them not as abstract and distant from ourselves, but as people whose steps are so intertwined with our own that we would realize that we inhabit not parallel realities but a shared reality?

How is it still possible that most of us, even when we stumble upon the tragic fate of others, do so as if they were stones, no more? This is a process called 'normalization'. If there ever was an 'anatomy of steps' that describes the process of normalization with surgical precision, it is to be found in Imre Kertész's semi-autobiographical novel *Fatelessness*.*

Kertész, a Hungarian Jew from Budapest, was deported when he was fifteen, first to Auschwitz and later to Buchenwald. He knew about the importance of steps. In the last chapter of *Fatelessness*, which describes the experiences of fifteen-year-old György Köves in the concentration camps of Auschwitz, Buchenwald and Zeitz, the protagonist is returning home after being freed from the horrors of Buchenwald. As he boards a tram, a man approaches him and asks: 'Have you come from the concentration camps?' and György automatically answers, 'Naturally.'[1]

The man, a journalist 'for a democratic paper', asks him about his experiences, suffering deprivation and hunger, to which the boy again answers, 'Naturally.'

'Why, my dear boy,' he exclaims on the verge of losing his patience, 'do you keep on saying "naturally", and always about things that are not at all natural?'

In the concentration camps, the boy explains, these things *were* natural. The man replies that concentration camps themselves are 'unnatural'. When the streetcar stops in a square and the boy gets off, the man does so too and suggests they sit down for a minute on a bench in the shade of some trees. The truth is, he remarks, that only now are the 'horrors really starting to come to light'. Turning to face the boy, he asks, 'Would you care to give an account of your experiences, young fellow?'

The boy is surprised and asks, 'But what about?'

'The hell of the camps,' the man replies. The boy retorts that he has nothing at all to say as he is not acquainted with hell and can't even imagine what it is like.

'Can we imagine a concentration camp as anything but a hell?' the journalist asks with puzzled astonishment.

The boy replies that everyone can think what they like about it, but

* I owe this point and elaboration to Aleksandra Savanović

he can only imagine a concentration camp, since he was acquainted with that, but not hell. Pressed further, he concedes that he can imagine it as 'a place where it is impossible to become bored'.

Shocked, the journalist demands why so. After a brief reflection, the boy comes up with one word: 'Time.'

Then, in a single extraordinary paragraph, Kertész explains what normalization means.

> I tried to explain how different it was, for example, to arrive in a not exactly opulent but still, on the whole, agreeable, neat, and clean station where everything becomes clear only gradually, sequentially, over time, step-by-step. By the time one has passed a given step, put it behind one, the next one is already there. By the time one knows everything, one has already understood it all. And while one is coming to understand everything, a person does not remain idle: he is already attending to his new business, living, acting, moving, carrying out each new demand at each new stage. Were it not for that sequencing in time, and were the entire knowledge to crash in upon a person on the spot, at one fell swoop, it might well be that neither one's brain nor one's ear would cope with it (. . .) For instance, I told him, I had seen prisoners who had already been – or to be more accurate were still – in concentration camps for four, six, even twelve years. Now, those people somehow had to fill each one of those four, six or twelve years, which in the latter case means twelve times three hundred and sixty-five days, which is to say twelve times three hundred and sixty-five times twenty-four times . . . and so on back, every second, every minute, every hour, every day of it, in its entirety.

What Kertész pinpoints is the way in which normalization functions step by step. It is inseparable from temporality, since it is precisely the passing of time which normalizes. 'Normalization' as a noun already implies that it is a becoming, a process, it normalizes the *nomos* (the ancient Greek term for 'law'). For Kertész, *nomos*, usually distinguished in ancient Greek philosophy from *physis* ('nature'), becomes in the case of concentration camps inseparable from *physis*: law becomes nature, and nature becomes law. This is the reason why at the start of their conversation, György's sole response is 'naturally'.

We have therefore to understand normalization as a process of 'naturalization' of the *nomos*, the becoming 'normal' of what was originally a 'norm', a set of prescribed, imposed rules (from the Latin *norma*).

In the eyes of its practitioners, the Holocaust was 'successful' precisely for this reason: because it turned a norm (the extermination of Jews based on the Nazi *Rassentheorie*, the doctrine asserting the superiority of the Aryan race, which claimed a spurious kind of scientific legitimacy) into something that is natural. It was the whole technological apparatus of the 'Final Solution' (from eugenics to the car-factory assembly line of the concentration camps) which produced this normalization, so to say, step by step. The temporality of normalization literally resides in the step, which should be understood as the real and precise measure towards any sort of totalitarianism: that is, each step that we take towards a point that becomes inevitable, normal – but that, had we chosen to take different steps, might not have become so.

Near the end of the book, György encounters other survivors, one of them explains that the only way they had managed to endure the camps was by 'trying to survive'. 'They too had taken one step at a time,' exclaims the boy. When the other survivors look puzzled, he relates to them how Auschwitz itself literally happened: *step by step*.

The boy recalls standing in the middle of a crowd of thousands being forced onto a train. He had between ten to twenty minutes before he reached the point where the decision was made for him: whether he would be sent directly to the gas chambers or would be afforded a temporary reprieve. Meanwhile, around him the queue was constantly moving and progressing; everyone was taking steps, bigger or smaller ones. The point is that Auschwitz didn't come about as a sort of natural phenomenon; rather, it was built by incremental steps.

'Every one of those minutes,' says Kertész at the end of *Fatelessness*, 'might in fact have brought something new. In reality it didn't, naturally, but still, one must acknowledge that it might have; when it comes down to it, each and every minute something else might have happened other than what actually did happen.'

Something else might have happened at Auschwitz – just as much as, let's suppose, at the very moment you're reading these lines. We have all taken steps in the past. And we are all taking steps into our future – steps whose direction we have the power to change.

If we want to avoid the possibility of future historians building some *Stolpersteine* to remind us of our current catastrophe, our task today is to be aware of the steps we are taking: to realize that the real question is not how did all this – Donald Trump, the disintegration of the EU, refugee camps, walls, climate change and new wars – come about, but what were the steps we ourselves took during all this.

On the day of Trump's inauguration in January 2017, one of the protesters at the 500,000-strong Women's March – the largest single-day protest in US history – carried a sign 'MAKE MARGARET ATWOOD FICTION AGAIN!' Not only was this the best encapsulation of our current predicament, but it warned again that totalitarianism is built step by step. What was once fiction is now becoming reality, not because of a sudden event or short circuit, but through many incremental steps.

In its depiction of a dystopian near future Atwood's *The Handmaid's Tale*, first published more than thirty years ago and newly popularized by the 2017 TV series of the same name, shows precisely how normalization is the first step towards totalitarianism.

In the book, the United States government has been overthrown by extremist Christian fundamentalists, who have rechristened the nation 'Republic of Gilead' and established a fundamentalist theocracy. Responding to environmental and health threats that have rendered most of the population infertile, Gilead segregates men and women into distinct social classes. In Gilead the women wear clothing and colours prescribed by their status in society: red for handmaids, blue for wives, green for Marthas – the domestic servants – and brown for aunts, the highest-ranking women in the Republic of Gilead, responsible for overseeing the training and indoctrination of the handmaids.

The protagonist, Offred – like all the fertile women remaining in Gilead – serves as a handmaid, belonging to a 'commander' and his wife; she acts as a sex slave and surrogate mother. Since Gilead strips handmaids of their original names, Offred is so called because her commander – who ceremonially rapes her monthly for the good of the state – is named Fred (she is his possession: literally, 'of-Fred').

Atwood details painstakingly the steps by which democracy is transformed into totalitarianism. In order to deprive women of their rights and establish a fundamentalist theocracy, the first move is to put in question women's property rights, then to freeze the bank accounts of all women; following this comes the classification into fertile and non-fertile women, later to be further subdivided into actual classes among women themselves. With each new step, it becomes ever more difficult to reverse what has been done: an inexorable march into the abyss.

Atwood constructed her dystopian fiction using historical precedents, digging at America's Puritan roots to build Gilead, and mining other parts from the past: the Nazi party's *Lebensborn* programme, designed to encourage a high birth rate among Aryan women; Nicolae Ceaușescu's fertility programmes; book burnings, group executions, sumptuary laws; religious iconography seen in enforced dress codes; state surveillance in China and East Germany. At the same time, Atwood did a huge amount of research on the resistance movements in various countries during the Second World War.

When the TV adaptation of *The Handmaid's Tale* was being shot, who would have said that a fictional series destined to come out in the era of Hillary Clinton, would only a few months later become the series about the reality of Donald Trump's presidency?

In a piece entitled 'What "The Handmaid's Tale" means in the age of Trump', published a few months into the Trump administration, Atwood recalled that back when she was writing the novel, the main premise seemed even to her fairly outrageous: 'Would I be able to persuade readers that the United States had suffered a coup that had transformed an erstwhile liberal democracy into a literal-minded theocratic dictatorship?'[2]

Now, this premise doesn't seem outrageous any more. Just four days after the Women's March, Trump signed an executive order to reinstate the 'Global Gag Rule', which was first introduced in 1984 by then-president Ronald Reagan, the same year *The Handmaid's Tale* was first published, and repealed in the interim. Also known as the 'Mexico City Policy', the legislation prohibits abortion counselling by any non-government international organization that receives US federal funding.

In April 2017 – the same day the US dropped MOAB, the 'mother of all bombs' (the largest non-nuclear bomb in America's arsenal) on the Afghan–Pakistan border with the goal of destroying tunnel complexes used by ISIL and ISIS[3] – Donald Trump quietly signed a law giving states the authority to halt federal funding of family-planning services to Planned Parenthood and other clinics that provide abortions. In other words, the legal right to have an abortion will soon be abolished across America under Donald Trump. Step by step.

Is *The Handmaid's Tale* a prediction, a prophecy? Margaret Atwood's answer to this is 'No'. It isn't a prediction, she writes, 'because predicting the future isn't really possible: there are too many variables and unforeseen possibilities. Let's say it's an anti-prediction: If this future can be described in detail, maybe it won't happen. But such wishful thinking cannot be depended on either.'[4]

'It can't happen here' – the most frequent phrase of our current denialism repeated as a mantra at cafés, dinners and parties – was made famous by Sinclair Lewis's 1935 novel of the same name, which depicted the slide of the United States into totalitarianism. Now, in the era of Trump and his European clones, the phrase needs inverting: it can happen everywhere, because it has already happened here!

Nowhere was this more true than in summer 2017, when thousands of white supremacists took over the Virginia town of Charlottesville for a 'Unite The Right' rally. Charlottesville became a sign from the future: a postmodern version of the Civil Rights era in which racism, sexism and antisemitism are still thriving in the United States. The white supremacists carried torches and chanted hateful slogans against the black, Jewish, immigrant and LGBTQ communities. A car ploughed into the crowd. A woman was murdered and nineteen protesters were injured.

Aren't the Charlottesville fascists (the so-called 'alt-right' – as if fascism has now become an 'alternative') an embodiment of Sinclair Lewis's nationwide brownshirt-style force, the Minute Men ('M.M.s'), or the militia forces that in Atwood's book would become part of the regular army and government of the United States? Why is it not so difficult any more to imagine something becoming reality which only a few years ago would have been dismissed as science fiction?

The answer, again, lies in the incremental steps. But it doesn't lie in some abstract steps, someone else's steps. It lies in our own steps.

Every day we can decide whether we want to make Margaret Atwood fiction again – or instead sleepwalk into a nightmare future in which fascism will be wrapped in the American – or Austrian, Czech, Polish, French, German, Croatian – flag. Every day we can decide whether we want to participate in the process of normalization, or whether we will be one step ahead and question what is portrayed as natural and slowly, step by step, starts to feel natural.

If we and our beloved ones don't want to end up as *Stolpersteine* for some future passer-by – unaware of the questions and doubts, fears and hopes we shared in the past as we walked on that same pavement – then we must take responsibility for our own steps.

INTERLUDE

Auschwitz
on the Beach?

At the end of August 2017, as half a continent was slowly waking from its summer slumber, one of Europe's finest art exhibitions, 'Documenta', held annually in the German city of Kassel, cancelled a forthcoming piece of performance art called 'Auschwitz on the Beach'. Perhaps unsurprisingly: after all, could there be a more provocative title? What on earth was it supposed to mean?

The planned performance drew on a piece of writing by the Italian philosopher Franco 'Bifo' Berardi, in which he compared the current plight of migrants stranded on the beaches of the Mediterranean to the horrors of the Second World War – or more precisely, the Holocaust. News of it caused outrage in Germany and in the end, due to public pressure, the curators decided to call it off.

In response, 'Bifo' stressed that the intention was not to cause offence nor to misuse the word 'Auschwitz', its unique meaning and implications. He wanted, rather, to provoke debate by referencing the 'heavy' meaning of Auschwitz, which in the public consciousness rightly remains a topic of the utmost gravity and seriousness.

In Germany, the mere announcement of 'Auschwitz on the Beach' had the desired effect: the main argument against the performance being that, in the words of the culture minister for the state of Hesse, Boris Rhein, 'any comparison to the Holocaust cannot be allowed as the crimes of the Nazis were unique'.[1]

A month before the performance was cancelled, Bifo outlined the notion behind it in a letter of resignation to the Democracy in Europe Movement 2025 (DiEM25). Founded in 2016 as a pan-European movement, DiEM25 currently has around 100,000 members, a membership which is convinced that only radical transnational politics can bring back democracy to Europe.

In his letter, Bifo asserted that there was no longer any such thing as democracy in Europe, a continent that had failed to overcome its history. Europe, he said, is 'nothing but nationalism, colonialism, capitalism and fascism'. In the Second World War, he continued, people had an excuse for not protesting against the deportations, segregations, torture and exterminations: few knew the reality of the death camps. Today, however, we have no excuse; we know what's going on around the Mediterranean: 'we know how deadly is the effect of European neglect and of the refusal to take responsibility for the migration wave that is a direct result of the wars provoked by two centuries of colonialism'. To stop the migration, Bifo stated, Europe is in the process of building concentration camps to hold refugees, and paying off the likes of Turkey, Libya and Egypt to do its dirty work on the Mediterranean coast, preventing people from setting out to Europe in the first place.

As long ago as 1991, Bifo wrote, when a ship loaded with 26,000 Albanians entered the Italian port of Brindisi, we knew that a great migration had begun. At that point, Europe had two paths available to it. The first: a route of open borders and the redistribution of resources in a process of reception and integration. The second: to reject, to dissuade, to make impossible the easy journey from Northern Africa to the coasts of Spain, Italy and Greece. Europe chose the second path. Daily, women, children and men are drowning. With few honourable exceptions – people now condemned for aiding and abetting illegal migrants – Europeans have refused to acknowledge their historical responsibility. All are complicit in what Bifo calls 'Auschwitz on the Beach'.

This is, obviously, a very dark assessment of Europe's predicament. Not only does Bifo intentionally compare the current refugee crisis to Auschwitz, but he holds Europe responsible for the refugees' 'extermination'. Stating that salt water has replaced Zyklon B is loaded – not to say, provocative. But Bifo knew precisely what he was doing. His intention, with this comparison, was to shock people into a public debate. Arguably, he succeeded.

Yet the public debate took an inevitable, predictable turn. Rather than sparking off a serious exchange of ideas on the refugee crisis and Europe's responsibility – both for those drowned in the Mediterranean Sea and those in concentration camps in Libya and elsewhere – the discussion was immediately drowned by a debate on the use of the word 'Auschwitz', and what can and can't be said in relation to it.

To put it in a nutshell: 'Auschwitz' and 'beach' can't go together. Their conjunction provokes an instant reaction, precisely because they signify something completely different: an oxymoron, two words which are purely oppositional. Even though unrealized, the impact of 'Auschwitz on the Beach' lies simply in its extreme dissonance. It dared to infect us, even if we succumbed to it unwillingly, with an image of Auschwitz on the beach, with a picture of Aylan Kurdi, the little Syrian boy who drowned in the Mediterranean in September 2015: his death not an isolated tragedy, but evidence of Europe's institutionalized rejection of migrants.

However, even if the intention behind 'Auschwitz on the Beach' was to break the strongest existing *Denkverbot* (beautiful German expression describing the 'prohibition to think'), Bifo himself couldn't do so. Perhaps the only person qualified to offer a way out of this closed loop of meaning is a Holocaust survivor.

In his 2001 piece 'Who owns Auschwitz?', Imre Kertész states – almost as if he were predicting the furore around Documenta in 2017 – that 'there is something shockingly ambiguous about the jealous way in which survivors insist on their exclusive rights to the Holocaust as intellectual property as though they'd come into possession of some great and unique secret, as though they were protecting some unheard-of treasure from decay and (especially) from willful damage'.[2]

Words that might be applied to the German debate around the cancelled performance of 'Auschwitz on the Beach'. Only it wasn't Holocaust survivors but the German media who acted as the *soi-disant* custodians of the Holocaust 'intellectual property': guarding it from misuse, not as survivors do through the strength of their memory, but through the vehemence of their condemnation of a performance which – even given the intensity of Bifo's language – wasn't intended to hurt the victims or survivors of the Holocaust. Rather, precisely the opposite: to warn that we might be – in Bifo's assessment, *we already are* – travelling in the direction of 'repeating Auschwitz'.

How right was Kertész when he said that he regards as 'kitsch' any representation of the Holocaust that is 'incapable of understanding or unwilling to understand the organic connection between our own deformed mode of life and the very possibility of the Holocaust'.[3] For Kertész, seeing Auschwitz as 'simply a matter concerning Germans and Jews and thereby reduced to something like the fatal incompatibility of two groups' is also kitsch: 'when the political and psychological anatomy of modern totalitarianism more generally is disregarded; when Auschwitz is not seen as a universal experience, but reduced to whatever immediately "hits the eye"'.[4]

This is precisely the point about 'Auschwitz on the Beach'. It was not remotely attempting to downplay the German or Jewish meanings of Auschwitz. It was, though, attempting to extrapolate, to articulate the universal nature of the horror of Auschwitz: to connect it to our own 'deformed mode of life' today, and the possibility that something like the Holocaust might happen again in another form.

Of course, it is a risk to describe the 30,000 people drowned in the Mediterranean Sea as a result of European policies, or the one million migrants detained in 'concentration camps' in Libya, as 'Auschwitz on the Beach'. Bifo's point, though, is that we should remember the famous saying *Nie wieder Auschwitz* ('Never again Auschwitz'). Even if the current crimes don't in themselves equate to Auschwitz, the aim behind Bifo's provocation (in the original Latin meaning, *provocatio*, 'a calling forth, a challenge') was to bring the ghastly potential of our current situation out into the open: Auschwitz might happen again.

Whether or not you agree with Bifo's dark autopsy of Europe, the point he makes in his resignation letter to DiEM25 (although he remains a member of the movement because DiEM25 didn't accept his resignation) brings us from the 'Occupation' (the first part of this book) to the 'Liberation' (the second part). It is the question of whether it is still possible to call ourselves Europeans if these horrors and atrocities *are* happening.

In his letter, Bifo renounced his European identity. Indeed, he declared that, if this is what it means to be European, to embrace a mentality that can turn a blind eye to these horrors, he has never been European. As a good reader of Austin's *How to Do Things with Words*,

Bifo surely knew that in declaring 'I am not European any more', he was making a 'performative utterance'. Such a statement is neither true nor false: it is, simply, a certain kind of action. In Bifo's case, it could be interpreted as a 'resignation' – or another provocation.[5]

If the assessment of Europe's – and more generally, the world's – situation today, as explored in the first part of this book, is at all correct, then the real question isn't so much whether or not another Auschwitz is possible, but how it can be avoided.

In the face of another Auschwitz (and by Auschwitz we mean the 'universal experience', as Kertész would call it), how can we get organized? If Auschwitz *can happen again*, what is our responsibility? How can we act in order to prevent it?

The first step is not to declare resignedly that we are 'not Europeans any more', but to do precisely the opposite. Yes, we know that to be 'European' immediately means – as Bifo pointed out in his letter – being weaned off at least five centuries of colonialism, capitalism and nationalism.[6] We know that 'Europe', leading to its dark logical conclusion, means 'Holocaust' as well. We know that there is no document of Europe which is not at the same time a document of barbarism.

And yet we also know that every document of Europe is a document of resistance as well. European values are not *either* enlightenment, humanism and universal human rights, *or* concentration camps, Zyklon B and the Holocaust. European values are *both*. To succumb to the belief that European values are encapsulated only by the first set of nouns is to fall into the trap of Eurocentrism and European exceptionalism – whose logical conclusion was that other horrific iteration of European values. But to subscribe to the view that European values are only concentration camps, Zyklon B and the Holocaust is to reject the emancipatory legacy which is also part of Europe and its history. Only by understanding that Europe is both simultaneously can we find a way out of our current predicament.

Back in summer 2011, in the wake of the Arab Spring, and with the Occupy movement flourishing all over Europe, I met in his Paris apartment someone who knew, who had intimately experienced both sets of European values: Stéphane Hessel, a concentration camp survivor and resistance fighter.

There we were, a 28-year-old European in conversation with a

94-year-old European; one depressed by Europe's situation and the other who still believed there was hope. But it wasn't the 94-year-old who was depressed and the 28-year-old hopeful. It was the other way round.

Until the very end of his life – he died a year later – Stéphane Hessel remained full of hope. When I suggested that his call to action, set out in his bestselling work *Indignez-vous!* (*Time for Outrage*), was utopian, he answered gently that resistance and the construction of a new world might be seen as such. However, 'when you're as old as I am, then you will have experienced that things which look like utopia can one day become reality: if the Nazi regime could be overthrown, if decolonization could take place, if Europe could be built – not successfully but certainly better than during the last centuries – then you can't but be hopeful'.[7]

As any young European should do, I quoted back at him Walter Benjamin's interpretation of Paul Klee's painting *Angelus Novus*, an image reproduced on the title page of Hessel's work.

In his 1940 essay 'Theses on the Philosophy of History', Benjamin – who owned Klee's original painting – described the 'New Angel': 'looking as though he is about to move away from something he is fixedly contemplating':

His eyes are staring, his mouth is open, his wings are spread. This is how one pictures the angel of history. His face is turned toward the past. Where we perceive a chain of events, he sees one single catastrophe which keeps piling wreckage upon wreckage and hurls it in front of his feet. The angel would like to stay, awaken the dead, and make whole what has been smashed. But a storm is blowing from Paradise; it has got caught in his wings with such violence that the angel can no longer close them. The storm irresistibly propels him into the future to which his back is turned, while the pile of debris before him grows skyward. This storm is what we call progress.[8]

So, I said to Hessel, if progress is nothing but an unceasing cycle of despair, then the 'Angel of History' is hardly the hopeful messenger that people might think it if they were to read *Indignez-vous!*

Extraordinarily enough, the young Stéphane Hessel met up with

Walter Benjamin, a family friend, in Marseille in 1940, just before Benjamin embarked on his escape from France across the Pyrenees with nothing but a gas mask and his toothbrush. As Hessel recalled, Benjamin was in despair; he himself, in his twenties, was hopeful. But as Hessel said to me seventy years later with determined calm: 'We can be in despair and we have many good reasons to be in despair, but we must fight against our own despair with hope.'

Throughout his life Hessel's actions gave shape to these words. Shortly after Walter Benjamin committed suicide in utter despair (*exaspération*) in Portbou, Hessel was fighting despair with hope (*aspiration*). Fleeing to London in 1941, he joined General Charles de Gaulle's Resistance, before returning to France to organize Resistance communication networks in advance of the 1944 Allied invasion. There, he was captured by the Gestapo and deported to the Buchenwald and Dora concentration camps. He managed to escape while being transferred to Bergen-Belsen, and reached Hanover, where he met the advancing Allied troops. After the war, he became a diplomat and was present at the drafting of the Universal Declaration of Human Rights. In October 2010 his small thirty-two-page pamphlet *Indignez-vous!* was published in a first edition of only 6,000 copies. Within ten weeks it had sold almost a million copies, in France alone.

In a world full of despair, this old, proud French Resistance fighter had reawakened hope. The 2011 Spanish protests and other examples of resistance, from cooperatives to communes, took the name *Indignados* ('the outraged') from the title of his work. That same year, the whole world – from Egypt and Tunisia, via Greece and Spain, to the United States – was occupying squares and streets, in the process bringing back hope.

All of which brings us back to 2017 and Bifo's resignation letter. Over the last six years the spring of hope has turned into the winter of despair. New political parties, founded in hope and optimism, have become like the old ones, lacking the strength to change the course of history. Meanwhile, the refugee crisis has deepened and new walls have been built; new wars are being waged and new fascisms articulated; as the European Union disintegrates, global instability is upon us. We are back in Marseille of 1940 with Walter Benjamin and Stéphane Hessel, at the crossroads of despair and hope.

Should we perhaps understand Bifo's resignation letter of 2017 as another form of Walter Benjamin's 'withdrawal': a desperate abandoning of any hope because there seems no way out? Or, perhaps Bifo thinks we need hope without optimism? Today, we are all faced with the same dilemma that confronted Benjamin and Hessel. It is not a matter of what is right and what is wrong (resignation or aspiration): both choices can be explained and understood. What matters is that we are aware of the choice, and that each choice also carries within it the possibility of making another choice.

Yet it would be wrong to think that the opposite of despair is optimism. Bifo's assessment of the current state of Europe – even his expression 'Auschwitz on the Beach' – is correct. Where he is wrong is in his embrace of *resignation* over *aspiration*. For Bifo, Europe is already lost, because the majority of the European population refuses to deal with its own historical responsibility. But it is not enough to resign. The only way to really take responsibility consists in rehabilitating hope – a much more radical hope than the naive notion of optimism. What we need more than ever today is hope without optimism. This is the only path from resistance to liberation.

PART TWO

The Sounds of Liberation

6

Summer in Athens: Hope without Optimism

If there ever was a recent summer of hope in Europe, it came in 2015, in Greece.

In early July that year, when Greece defaulted on its debt of €1.6 billion to the International Monetary Fund (IMF) and the European Central Bank (ECB), both institutions refused to accept Greek bonds as collateral for loans to Greek commercial banks. As a result, Greece was forced to impose capital controls, which in practice meant control over transfers from Greek banks to foreign banks and a limit of €60 per day on cash withdrawals for Greek citizens, to avoid an uncontrolled run on the banks and a complete collapse of the Greek banking system. Yet during these hot weeks the streets of Athens were not full of despair, but full of hope. For the first time after years of austerity and debt, the Greek *demos* felt as if a different future could be glimpsed on the horizon, as if there might finally be a chance for *democracy*.

In the early morning of 27 June 2015, Prime Minister Alexis Tsipras had announced a referendum on whether or not Greece should accept the bailout conditions proposed by the so-called 'Troika' (the European Commission, the International Monetary Fund and the European Central Bank). The first referendum to be held since the republic referendum of 1974, it was the only one in modern Greek history not to concern the form of government. It was also the first referendum in the EU's history on whether a member state should accept the conditions of a financial bailout.

At first glance, it seemed as if nothing had happened since the last time I was in Athens the previous year. At that time Syriza, the radical left party opposed to the EU's austerity politics, had not yet taken power and no one could even have imagined the events of

January to July 2015, the 'Greek Spring'.[1] Now, it's business as usual. One of the main shopping streets, Ermou, which runs from the famous Kerameikos below the Acropolis to Syntagma Square, where the Greek Parliament is based and which is a magnet for protest, is full of crowds shopping. Stores are heaving, *tavernas* and cafés packed.

However, something is different.

Every corner of Athens – every park, every square, every kiosk, even the air – is heavy with tension. Heated debates break out, while spontaneous protests, political gatherings and street theatre have become part of everyday life. A short distance from Syntagma Square, the students have placed a flag at the National Academy building with the inscription 'We vote "against" at the referendum on Sunday. We say OXI [NO] to EU and ECB blackmail.' On the walls of the ministry of finance there is another slogan, this time in English: 'No to blackmail and austerity'. The finance minister Yanis Varoufakis, who would become a figurehead of the fight against austerity throughout Europe, later stated it was an initiative of the trade unionists.

On radio and TV, in the papers, you can't escape from politics. OXI posters plaster the city, the word stamped across the face of the German finance minister Wolfgang Schäuble, one of Europe's leading proponents of austerity politics; OXI is daubed on banks throughout the centre of Athens. Most of them are closed.

For Greeks, OXI has a historical resonance that can be traced back to 28 October 1940. Mussolini had issued an ultimatum demanding that Greece allow Axis forces to enter the country and occupy strategic locations or face war. Greece said no (*oxi*) to the occupier. Now, despite the ubiquity of Schäuble's face on the posters, it is not only Germany which is perceived as the new 'occupier' of Greece – and I use the word advisedly: in April 2015, the Greek government demanded almost €279 billion in war reparations from the German government for the Nazi occupation during the Second World War, a request which was never met. At the end of June that year, leaked IMF documents revealed that the institution, notorious for its 'shock therapy' and austerity measures, admitted that even if Greece accepted the Troika's new package of measures and reforms, it would still not be able to repay its debt – which at the time stood at 175 per cent of GDP.[2] In fact, even if Greece experienced some surreal level of economic growth over the next fifteen years, debt would still be higher than 110 per cent of GDP (the target set by the Eurogroup of finance ministers in November 2012).

A day after these IMF documents were leaked, on 1 July 2015, Greece became the first European country not to pay its debts to the International Monetary Fund.[3] If you follow the mainstream global media, you'd be forgiven for thinking that there was chaos in Athens as a result. But this is fake news *avant la lettre*. There is no chaos: queues at some ATMs, yes, but no queues at others; supermarkets – contrary to reports – are stocked as usual. Life continues. There is some apprehension that Greek banks might run out of money if the referendum result returned OXI, but the streets of Athens themselves are filled with hope. Not optimism – there is none of that – but hope.

In the run-up to the referendum, at a massive public gathering of 50,000 people in front of the Greek Parliament in a baking Syntagma Square, Alexis Tsipras declared emphatically that 'democracy cannot be blackmailed'; 50,000 Greeks supported him at Syntagma Square. For his part, Yanis Varoufakis, who had become the main enemy of the Eurogroup, defiantly rejected their bailout conditions (even calling the methods of the Troika 'financial water-boarding').[4]

Two days after the demonstration, on 5 July, 61 per cent of Greeks voted OXI, rejecting the EU's austerity measures – and, by extension, membership of the EU itself. Athens celebrated as though Greece had won the World Cup: squares, terraces and balconies turned into venues for all-night parties.

But the hangover came quickly. The following morning Yanis Varoufakis suddenly resigned.[5] In the meantime, Tsipras had prepared a new agreement proposal, the so-called 'Third Memorandum' (the third bailout package for Greece) that offered Greece a new loan of €86 billion while demanding the privatization of €50 billion of state assets, along with structural adjustments to the pension system and labour market. A few days later, the Greek Parliament voted in favour of the new agreement, overturning the referendum result.

Shortly after, somebody added Tsipras's name to Wikipedia in the 'Greek Tragedy' category: 'The most important authors of Greek tragedy are Aeschylus, Sophocles, Euripides and . . . Tsipras.' This tragic quip was removed within an hour, yet it said something about how people saw the Greek Parliament's vote as a betrayal: how easily 'OXI' ('No' to austerity) can be transformed into 'NAI' ('Yes' to austerity), and how easily hope can be turned into melancholy.[6]

Representing not only hope for Greece but Europe as a whole, Syriza and Tsipras had come to power on a promise to end austerity and renegotiate the national debt, yet they had agreed to accept a new loan and were promising to implement further austerity. Overnight the streets, previously overflowing with joyous Greeks, emptied and fell silent.

During these melancholic days, I'm invited to a theatre play taking place in an old hangar at the port of Piraeus. The city is itself a tragic reminder of Greece's problems. Since its debt crisis began in late 2009, the Greek government planned to privatize several state-owned assets in order to repay its debts; one of them being Piraeus. Following the new agreement with the Troika, in 2016 the port was sold to the Chinese state-owned company COSCO, with a 51 per cent stake and option to acquire the remaining share. From being one of Europe's biggest ports, it became one of China's most important strategic ports in Europe. As we enter the hangar, the first thing I notice is a banner, a backdrop to the stage, proclaiming the message: 'Your melancholia is a luxury'. Very quickly, the play's director had worked out the dangers of sinking into despair after the defeat represented by Syriza's capitulation to the EU.

Yet now, after all the emancipatory struggles and transformative events that took place throughout the world from the Arab Spring to Occupy Wall Street, from Gezi Park to Sarajevo, from Hamburg to Barcelona – we bear witness precisely to a prevailing melancholy, a widely shared resignation in the face of multiple defeats, and a growing acceptance even among the most radical progressives that Margaret Thatcher was actually right when she said that 'There is no alternative.'

The story goes like this. Back in late 2002, Lady Thatcher was doing the rounds at a reception when one of the guests asked her what her greatest achievement was. She promptly replied, 'Tony Blair and New Labour. We forced our opponents to change their minds.' She was right. The true triumph comes when the enemy starts to adopt the ideology and economic policies to which they were previously opposed. The true triumph of Thatcher's dictum is that not even the left believes there really *is* an alternative any more.

In recent years this melancholia has swept the world like a contagion. Although the immense enthusiasm and massive demonstrations on the streets and squares from 2011 to 2015 marked the definitive end of Fukuyama's 'End of History', the horizontal movements either faded away and were unable to tackle the power of the establishment (Occupy Wall Street); or were immediately replaced by new authoritarian or neoliberal regimes (the Egyptian Spring); or were soon forced to accept TINA – 'There is no alternative' (Syriza in Greece after the signing of the Third Memorandum); or have been unable to take power yet (Podemos in Spain or the Labour Party in Britain).

Now, the spirit of Thatcher seems to haunt us again: this time suffused with a sense of the apocalyptic narrative, best summed up in Fredric Jameson's words, 'it is easier to imagine the end of the world than the end of capitalism'. The prevailing feeling among those who occupied the squares and streets, who protested or joined new political parties, who came close to power or are – like Syriza – still in power is the 'illness' beautifully described by Walter Benjamin as 'left-wing melancholy'.[7]

If we want to understand what left-wing melancholy means, we have first to understand the psychoanalytical difference between 'mourning' and 'melancholy'. Both derive from the loss or absence of a beloved object (in our case, the lost battles of the Greek Spring, Occupy Wall Street, Indignados, Arab Spring, Gezi Park or Syriza . . .), but differ in their responses. In mourning, a person eventually succeeds in overcoming the grief of a loss (the death of a loved one; divorce; a failed revolution and so on), finally separating themselves from this lost possession (person, value, ideal). The melancholic subject, on the other hand, remains narcissistically identified with their lost beloved object. It's melancholy from which most of the left seems to be suffering, utterly unable to move forward.

But what if this prevailing melancholy, this loss, can be transformed into something productive and constructive? The Italian historian Enzo Traverso makes this point in his important book *Left-Wing Melancholia*, a sort of theoretical and political self-help manual for all leftist – and other – melancholics.

For Traverso, 'left melancholy' is the result of an impossible mourning: 'communism is both a finished experience and an irreplaceable loss, in the age in which the end of utopias obstructs the separation from the lost beloved ideal as well as a libidinal transfer toward a new object of love'.[8]

Is melancholy therefore only a 'luxury' – as the Greek play in Piraeus after the OXI referendum warned us – or is it even – as the political theorist Wendy Brown puts it – a 'conservative tendency' without any transformative potential?[9] For Traverso, it is precisely this conservative tendency that could also be viewed as a form of resistance against demission and betrayal of the lost struggles which give birth to this melancholy. Even if the twenty-first century was heralded by the collapse of the communist utopia (the end of the Cold War and the fall of the Berlin Wall marking the end of the 'really existing socialism' of the twentieth century), even if the very word 'utopia' disappeared in the real existing dystopia, for Traverso it is melancholy, not mourning, that is truly transformative. Because of the end of utopias, successful mourning might also result in identification with the enemy: the lost struggles replaced by accepted capitalism. If, as Thatcher warned us, there is no alternative, the refusal to believe in the possibility of an alternative inevitably results in a disenchanted acceptance of global capitalism. By contrast, melancholy becomes the obstinate refusal of any compromise with the enemy. Moreover, we could see it as a necessary premise of a mourning process, a step that precedes and allows mourning in order to make us active again, instead of paralysing us.

To translate this back into the experiences of the Greek Spring – or any other occupation and protest movement from the last decade – left melancholy does not necessarily mean nostalgia for the real Syriza (before it signed the Third Memorandum); rather, it means that the lost object (the Greek Spring) can still be the very means of emancipation. In this view, as Traverso notes, melancholy means memory and awareness of the potentialities of the past, 'a fidelity to the emancipatory promises of revolution, not to its consequences'.[10]

In other words, we must constantly remind ourselves that there are no final defeats. In January 1919, Rosa Luxemburg was beaten to death with rifle butts, her body thrown into the Berliner Landwehrkanal. Shortly before her murder, Rosa wrote the piece that would become her last message, celebrating defeat with words announcing a future victory:

The whole road of socialism – so far as revolutionary struggles are concerned – is paved with nothing but thunderous defeats. Yet, at the same time, history marches inexorably, step by step, toward final victory! Where would we be today *without* those 'defeats', from which we draw historical experience, understanding, power and idealism? Today, as we advance into the final battle of the proletarian class war, we stand on the foundation of those very defeats; and we cannot do without *any* of them, because each one contributes to our strength and understanding.[11]

Instead of understanding melancholy as something negative, as a nostalgic look into the past which can't be processed through mourning, maybe the time has come to rehabilitate melancholy in the way Traverso suggests: as something that actually carries an emancipatory potential. Such melancholy wouldn't mean grieving over lost opportunities, but creating an emancipatory crack in the current dystopia precisely by remembering those opportunities and fulfilling hitherto unrealized potential. However, where Rosa Luxemburg is not quite right is in her reference to the 'final victory'. There is, it is true, no victory without those 'defeats'; equally, and this is the hope without optimism, there can be no final victory.

Back to the future: it is almost a hundred years since Rosa Luxemburg uttered her words about the importance of defeats and I am flying to Boston to meet Noam Chomsky, the great American linguist and social critic. Chomsky became political early in life: he wrote his first article at the age of ten, following the fall of Barcelona to Francisco Franco's fascist army in December 1938. In the 1960s Chomsky, a vocal opponent of the Vietnam War, was arrested several times, and even ended up on Richard Nixon's 'Enemies List'. During the Reagan years, he was active in the movement against America's increased military interventions in Central America, and in 1988 he visited the Palestinian territories to witness the impact of US-backed Israeli military occupation there. With the same clarity and defiance, he criticized US imperialism and exceptionalism during the Clinton and Bush years. When in 2001 the World Social Forum was founded in Brazil, Chomsky visited Porto Alegre and became one of the first supporters of this global movement. If there is someone whose own life was part of the struggles of the twentieth and early twenty-first centuries, it is without any doubt Noam Chomsky.

For my generation, which was gaining its political subjectivity in the aftermath of the Yugoslav wars, Noam Chomsky has been a key figure. The internet era was just at the beginning, and we didn't as yet know much about his work in linguistics, but as teenagers, at underground punk and hardcore concerts, we were exchanging his early translations of political texts (together with those of anarchist authors such as Bakunin, Kropotkin, Proudhon, Emma Goldman), which pointed towards a way out of the prevailing nationalism and neoliberalism that in the 1990s were conquering what was once known as Yugoslavia. As the new millennium dawned, I was finally discovering Chomsky's linguistic work as a student of linguistics and philosophy at the Zagreb Faculty of Philosophy, and decided to send him my first email. To my surprise, his answer arrived hours later.

Now, after eighteen years of digital friendship, I finally had the chance to meet Chomsky in person. Late September 2016 and the US election was in full swing. The day before I arrived, the presidential debate between Hillary Clinton and Donald Trump had been watched by 84 million Americans, breaking a thirty-six-year record (the debate between Jimmy Carter and Ronald Reagan). In the taxi I can hear Donald Trump on the radio once again promising to build a huge wall along the Mexican border to stop illegal immigration. The last time I was in the US, in 2011, I visited Occupy Wall Street in New York's Zuccotti Park. This time, there was no hope in the air, only a choice between Hillary Clinton and Donald Trump.

So, naturally, my first question to Chomsky was about the defeats we suffered since all the springs: from Occupy to the massive uprisings at Tahrir Square and Syntagma Square. His reply was characteristically measured: 'if you look back in history, those movements that succeeded seem like those who have failed or didn't succeed to achieve their goals', yet 'they left traces and legacies that are bringing us forwards'. The first example he named was the abolition of slavery. If you looked at abolitionism in 1850, you might have said it failed, yet the traces left by the movement served as the foundation for a struggle that led to the abolition of slavery. The same goes for the struggle for women's rights and other movements. If a movement fails today, said Chomsky, it nevertheless has an impact on the general consciousness, on our understanding of the world – even on institutional structures. And the next example he used was the Occupy movement. 'You can say that this movement failed because it did not abolish financial institutions, but that was the very basis for the phenomenon of Bernie Sanders, who was pretty close to taking over one of the two US capitalist parties.[12]

Chomsky is right. But the very fact that there is no such thing as a final defeat means that there is also no final victory. Even though myriad successful struggles have contributed – and continue to contribute – to the creation of a fairer society based on emancipation of the oppressed, it doesn't mean that we won't soon be witnessing the violence of Charlottesville or the Hamburg G20 in other cities and countries, or that even the United States might not turn into a totalitarian dystopia similar to a combination of *The Handmaid's Tale* and *The Circle*. Even if the worldwide Occupy movements have contributed to the creation of cooperatives and the emergence of alternative economies (Greece, Spain), even if they lead to the formation of new political parties (Syriza, Podemos) and even if some of those parties have taken power (Syriza, Barcelona en Comú – the movement currently governing Barcelona), this doesn't mean that there won't be new defeats or that – to echo Lenin's famous phrase – one step forward can't again become two steps back. Understanding this is what hope without optimism means.

The phrase was originally coined by Terry Eagleton in 2014 in a series of lectures given – ironically, in light of later events – in Charlottesville. Dismissing optimism as a typical privilege of the ruling classes, Eagleton argued that its refutation is an essential condition of political change. Instead of optimism – a naive belief that things will get better – we need hope without optimism. Things probably won't get better, but if we are able to project ourselves into a possible, graspable future then it can become, as Eagleton says, 'in some shadowy sense already present'.[13] This is the reason why such hope without optimism can be born only out of utter hopelessness, or what Slavoj Žižek in his most recent work called 'the courage of hopelessness'.[14]

Terry Eagleton puts it this way:

> Not to succeed in the end is not necessarily to have failed, any more than it is true that all's well that ends well. It is only the lure of teleology that persuades us of this fallacy. Even if history were to fall into utter ruin, it would be a matter for despair only if that catastrophe were predestined; and even then it is possible, like many a tragic protagonist, to pluck value from combating the inevitable. Indeed, unless one combats the inevitable, one will never know how inevitable it was in the first place. The truth, however, is that catastrophe is not written into the march of history, any more than hope is. However desolate the future may prove, it might always have been different. The contingency that can make for misfortune can also make for success.[15]

In this view – to return to Athens in the hot summer of 2015 – the fact that the Greek Spring didn't succeed doesn't mean that the movement is over. The potentiality is still here: the Greeks continue to fight against the Third Memorandum and Syriza's subsequent implementation of austerity and sale of state assets. Even though much of the population remains despairing, the struggle continues – precisely because there is a complete lack of hope in the current system, and no belief that even a new government could renegotiate the bailout conditions of international financial institutions. In other words, it is out of these defeats that we must learn and build something different: a stronger movement. And so, the struggle goes on: from protests to general strikes, from refugee solidarity movements to cooperative markets. It is this hope without optimism that can carry us into the future, because it salvages what has passed not as something that has to be repeated, but as a potential that might lead in new directions and that can still – if we keep constantly in mind the lesson that there is no final defeat – change the present.

This is exactly what is happening during our long winter of melancholy in Europe. From France to Italy, from Greece to Spain, new models of alternative economies are being developed, new models of governance at the local and municipal level are being set up from Barcelona to Naples, and new forms of life outside capitalism are being created. But can there really be an 'outside'?

7

Islands Outside Capitalism?

It is late summer of 2016. I am leaving Barcelona and heading into the country to visit one of the many communes which, since the outbreak of the financial crisis in 2008, have sprung up throughout Catalonia. Tired of inhabiting a failed system, weighed down by debt, evictions and rising poverty, many local people, mostly young, started to seek out new ways of living that defy the dictum that there is no alternative.

After an hour and a half of driving through rugged hills, I reach the Pujarnol valley. We're only fifteen minutes from the town of Banyoles and half an hour from the regional capital of Girona, but it feels isolated, a different world. Based in a thousand-year-old stone house, a Catalan *masia*, surrounded by 70 acres of land, the Som Comunitat was launched in 2011 as an 'autonomous project of collective initiative' of the Catalan Integral Cooperative (CIC), one of the most interesting cooperative projects to spring up during our age of crisis, seeking to generate a self-managed, post-capitalist society based on P2P (peer to peer) principles and environmental and social projects.[1] It's a small community of people who live and work according to the principles of the integral revolution ('integral' in the sense of holistic or complete, something which concerns every single facet of life) and agro-ecology (ecological principles and processes applied to agricultural production systems).

As in the Spanish Civil War, when communes in revolutionary Catalonia functioned as liberated zones and worked on entirely anarchist principles, Som Comunitat has established itself as an autonomous and self-sustainable community, which is at the same time inside and outside the system: 'inside' inasmuch as it is based in Catalonia and global and European developments are reflected both on the local and even micro-local levels (the economic and social catastrophe in Spain, the Catalan independence referendum, the Eurozone's crisis and so on); 'outside' because its members have succeeded in building an autonomous system which can be understood as a new form of living, or something that we might call an 'ethico-system'.

Entering the old house, I was invited into a spacious dining room where we were served a delicious Moroccan couscous. Nine people were gathered at a big table. Mostly from different regions of Spain, they combined varied forms of experience and expertise: in protest movements, in ecological agriculture, in computer programming; others were just born in the commune. Som Comunitat felt to me instantly like a real 'heterotopia'.

In the commune they share everything: property is communal. Their aim is to move away from a capitalist economy based on private incomes and private profits, to a new kind of economy based on the 'commons' (resources that are accessible and organized by all members of society). During the last decade many movements advocating the commons, most notably the 'free software' movement, succeeded in creating tools to run small-scale (micro-local and local) alternative economies. Som Comunitat is trying to achieve something more ambitious: to organize a whole system or way of living related to the commons. Not only is the economy of the *masia* run collectively, so is their very way of life.

The group assembles once a week, and its members make decisions by consensus about the management of the commune. Routine tasks like cooking or cleaning are assigned by a system of job rotation, so that all members participate equally, while each pays €150 a month into the common budget. The monthly rent for the 600-square-metre stone house is only €1,000, since it was leased to the CIC for a period of fifteen years with the proviso that the cooperative will repair those parts of the *masia* which are in bad condition.

I ask them, playing devil's advocate, if their new lives aren't a kind of escapism – are they really changing society?

Suddenly everyone at the table wants to speak. They are emphatic that this is no escape from society. They prefer life among nature, convinced that cities are already overcrowded and designed a priori to prevent new ways of living. Instead of being forced to conform to the existing debt economy, they run their own alternative economy – but with one foot inside the existing structures of society.

But look at Europe, I reply. Things are changing fast. Isn't your creation of society going rather slowly?

Vamos lentos, one of the communards replies, *porque vamos lejos*. It's the Zapatista motto: 'We walk slow, because we walk far.' Its meaning isn't connected only to temporality (a time that goes beyond the accelerated global capitalism and its production of time itself), but to the Zapatista maxim *caminando preguntamos* ('as we walk we ask questions'), stressing the importance of being focused not so much on the final outcome, but on the experience of creation itself: not so much on changing a society which is supposedly out there (like the 'truth' in *X-Files*, which is never to be found), but on questioning and changing oneself in order to create a new society. In this, Som Comunitat draws on both the Catalan anarchist tradition and the experiences of various contemporary commons movements. Or as the Spanish poet Antonio Machado put it: 'Traveller, there is no path. The path is made by walking.'

Nevertheless, the question which can't be avoided – even in the tranquillity and gentle breezes of the Pujarnol valley – is whether the model of the commune can be scaled onto the rest of society. Even if this proves possible, won't it be too slow compared to the way global capitalism is radically transforming not only economic relations but also interpersonal relations and even the idea of the human self? What about the penetration of Silicon Valley into every corner of our lives, and the commodification of human relationships through Airbnb, Uber, Facebook; what about the refugee crisis and the austerity measures imposed throughout Europe; what about Donald Trump and the increased possibility of nuclear war or ecological disaster; what about the wars in the Middle East and Africa; what about new walls going up in Hungary or Mexico? Is it possible to create a parallel society in embryo while the rest of the population is suffocating? What if current forms of capitalism morph into some new kind of fascism? Surely the communards will have to take action to resist it – or even to confront it head on?

After I've finished bombarding the group with questions, one of the communards takes me to another room and shows me, without much explanation, an internet router. The message is clear: the commune is not outside society.

Som Comunitat's relationship with the CIC is not one of economic dependency, but a collaboration based on common principles. In order to sustain itself, the commune depends on income from three main sources: it produces and sells products – such as falafel, sauces (e.g. ketchup), veggie burgers and hummus – through the local eco-network in Girona and the CIC; it organizes events, such as jam sessions on Fridays; and it provides bed and breakfast accommodation for travellers who wish to spend a few days at the old stone house.

The CIC comprises more than 600 projects and businesses across Catalonia, including freelancers, companies, farms, residences and Calafou, a post-capitalist eco-industrial colony in the ruins of a 28,000-square-metre abandoned textile works just outside the village of Valbona. It was co-founded by Enric Durán, who was still on the run from Interpol and living as a fugitive outside Spain at the time we visited Som Comunitat.[2]

Back in September 2008, as Spain's economy collapsed, Durán became notorious overnight when he announced that he had robbed the Spanish banking system of nearly €500,000. Over the previous two years, he had taken out sixty-eight personal loans, distributing the funds to a variety of activist movements and social causes.

The mainstream media inevitably dubbed Durán the 'Robin Hood of the bank', though his inspiration came from other anarchists and revolutionary social movements. One influential figure for Durán was Basque anarchist Lucio Urtubia, who used travellers' cheques to orchestrate a multimillion-dollar fraud against Citibank in the 1970s, an action that caused Citibank's stocks to plummet. Durán followed Urtubia in using the money to finance a host of revolutionary and anarchist organizations but, unlike him, made his action public precisely to defend the legitimacy of what he did. Another inspiration for Durán was the Zapatista movement, which practises autonomy by 'not accepting power, and not trying to justify something before those from above'.

Since 2011 the CIC has succeeded in building an alternative economy based on mutual credit, reputation systems and crypto-currencies, leading to the launch in summer 2017 of the first cooperative block-chain called 'FairCoin'.

Unlike Bitcoin, FairCoin creates an algorithm based on mining processes that relies on a proof of cooperation. Usually when a Bit-coin blockchain transaction is carried out it is grouped together in a cryptographically protected block with other transactions that have occurred around the same time. The members in the network with high levels of computing power, known as 'miners', then compete to validate the transactions by solving complex coded problems. The first miner to solve the problems and validate the block receives a reward in Bitcoins. A profound belief of FairCoin is that cooperation is more efficient than competition. In other words, the cooperative is always already a commune if it wants to be a truly radical coopera-tive (because the cooperation is based on commons, not on private property or accumulation of capital, which is the case with Bitcoin).

Leaving behind the world of Som Comunitat, an existing parallel reality based on equality and mutual respect, we headed back to Barcelona. Our re-entry into the world of competition was rendered even more stark as we got caught in traffic. It brought to mind Jean-Luc Godard's 1967 film *Weekend*, probably one of the greatest car movies of all time, in which French bourgeois society starts to col-lapse under the weight of its own consumer drives. 'My Hermès handbag!' a woman cries as she watches her car burn in a three-way pile-up engulfed in flames . . .

As we sat gridlocked in the Barcelona traffic, the usual arsenal of counter-arguments to the communes ('what about this?', 'why aren't you this or that?', 'what about surplus value?' and so on) didn't sound so convincing any more. If our civilization is already heading towards a never-ending nightmare of gridlock and violence, perhaps these new cooperatives and communes, with their social crypto-currencies and alternative economies, with their communal decision-making and economy of commons, will indeed be among the rare sustainable forms of society after the collapse of civilization.

Precisely this argument is being put forward by the radical theory and practice of another commune, lying in an almost inaccessible mountain village in one of France's least populated areas, the 'Tar-nac' group.

In the same way that Spanish cooperatives and communes draw their inspiration from revolutionary Catalonia, this mountainous area has a tradition of rural resistance and autonomy dating back to the French Revolution. When the Nazis invaded France in 1940, the mountains and woods of the Corrèze region harboured so many members of the French Resistance that the invading Wehrmacht referred to the area as 'Little Russia'. It is precisely this part of Vichy France which, similarly to the autonomous zones in revolutionary Catalonia, had its own liberated territories that were never successfully occupied by the Nazis during the Second World War.

The Tarnac experience started in 2005 when a group of friends – centred on *Tiqqun*, a radical philosophy magazine influenced by post-situationism, autonomy and the works of Michel Foucault, Gilles Deleuze and Giorgio Agamben – set up a commune in the village of Tarnac in the Corrèze department. Like Som Comunitat, Tarnac soon transformed itself into an autonomous zone, at the same time inside and outside the system. The communards bought a disused farmhouse, planted a garden and began to raise livestock. Soon they took over the operation of a failing bar and general store, the only two businesses in the town, and ran them as volunteer collectives. And again, eco-system and ethico-system, alternative economy and a new way of living, went hand in hand.

The Tarnac farm rose to global prominence in November 2008 when *gendarmes* raided it and arrested nine residents in connection with an alleged TGV sabotage. Steel rods had been placed on overhead power cables on three railway lines, forcing the cancellation of more than a hundred trains and stranding some 20,000 passengers.[3] The arrests were publicly endorsed by Interior Minister Michèle Alliot-Marie, who described the suspects as 'an anarcho-autonomist cell'.

The complicated legal proceedings of the 'Tarnac affair' dragged on for seven years before terrorism charges against the Tarnac Nine were dropped in August 2015, a judgment upheld by the Supreme Court in January 2017. Finally, fifteen months later, after ten long years, the defendants were acquitted on all other charges on 12 April 2018. The French judges described the idea of the Tarnac Nine belonging to a left-wing 'anarchist terror cell' as fiction.[4]

Commenting on the trial, Italian philosopher Giorgio Agamben observed that

> the only possible conclusion to this shadowy affair is that those engaged in activism against the (in any case debatable) way social and economic problems are managed today are considered *ipso facto* as potential terrorists, when not even one act can justify this accusation. We must have the courage to say with clarity that today, numerous European countries (in particular France and Italy) have introduced laws and police measures that we would previously have judged barbaric and anti-democratic, and that these are no less extreme than those put into effect in Italy under fascism.[5]

The centrepiece of evidence in this anti-terrorism case was the now legendary book *L'insurrection qui vient* (*The Coming Insurrection*), which sketched a plan for revolution based on the formation of communes and by promoting insurrections worldwide, written by the so-called 'Invisible Committee', the *nom de plume* of anonymous authors associated with the Tarnac Nine group.

Had we asked the Tarnac Nine the question we posed to the Catalan communards, 'if we look at France today, let alone the rest of Europe, the decaying and militarized cities, the destroyed nature and prevailing apocalyptic feeling, isn't this creation of society going too slow?', they would have probably answered in the manner of *The Coming Insurrection*:

> It's useless to wait for a breakthrough, for the revolution, the nuclear apocalypse or a social movement. To go on waiting is madness. The catastrophe is not coming, it is here. We are already situated within the collapse of a civilization. It is within this reality that we must choose sides.[6]

This is the best possible answer to the false opposition of the 'fetishist denialism' ('we know perfectly well that the apocalypse is coming, but we continue with our lives as usual') and 'fetishist apocalypticism' ('we know very well that the apocalypse is coming, so we prepare for it'), and a call to awake from the prevailing apocalyptic *zeitgeist*. The question, in the words of *The Coming Insurrection*, is no longer when the catastrophe will happen, and what will happen when it happens. The more pertinent – and constructive – question is: what if the apocalypse is already taking place around us? Instead of waiting for the Messiah – a devotion and illness very well established among the left-wing intelligentsia – what the Invisible Committee proposes as the main task of today is both to focus on local struggles and to question the very temporality of 'capitalist realism', the prevailing feeling that the apocalypse is yet to come and that there is no alternative, while in fact it is happening now and the alternative has to be built on its ruins.

It is no wonder that, after *The Coming Insurrection* and *To Our Friends* (a reflection on, and extension of, the ideas laid out in their first volume), the Invisible Committee published a book entitled simply *Now*, whose chief argument is that we have to break from the constant impulse towards *tomorrow*, because this waiting for the future is nothing else but the maintenance of order, a sentiment of powerlessness which renders passive and numbs the whole population. For the Invisible Committee, there never was, there is not and there never will be anything but the *now*.

What both the Catalan and the French communes exemplify is precisely this radical transformation of temporality. Instead of waiting either for the coming apocalypse or the never-coming revolution, the various communes all around Europe – from Som Comunitat to Tarnac – are turning upside down the truly reactionary habit of postponing radical change. Instead of fantasizing about the right moment to bring about such change, when circumstances will be ripe and conditions ideal, the new society must be built now. One of the most important lessons of the Yugoslav Partisan movement during the Second World War was the truly dialectical point that there is never a moment when all conditions for making revolution exist. It is only by making the revolution that the conditions can be created. It is the revolution itself that creates its own conditions.

Or as the Invisible Committee puts it in *Now*:

> Everyone sees that this civilization is like a train heading towards the abyss, and that accelerates. The more it accelerates, the more are heard

the drunken hysterical hoorays from the discotheque car. You would have to lend an ear to detect the petrified silence of rational spirits who no longer understand anything, of those anguished who bite their nails and the false accent of serenity in the intermittent exclamations of those who play cards, waiting. Internally, many people have chosen to jump from the train, but they remain on the footboard. They are still beset by so many things. And they feel so held because they have made the choice, but the decision is lacking. For it is the decision that traces in the present the manner and the possibility of acting, of taking a jump that is not into the void. This decision, it is that of the deserter, that of stepping out of the rank, that of organizing oneself, that of secession, be it imperceptibly, but in all cases, *now*.[7]

Is the commune the answer to our apocalyptic times? With its central insistence on autonomy and self-management, it undoubtedly comes closest in the creation of new ways of living. By breaking with economic dependency and political subjugation and opposing the prevailing consensus, the commune creates the foundations of a new society. If there is a lesson to be learnt from Som Comunitat and Tarnac, it is this far-reaching deconstruction of the left-wing sickness called 'the right moment'.

Yet there are many unresolved questions. Will the experience of these communes always be purely local, or can it be translated into different contexts? Can it become an efficient way of organizing and living, even for those in non-rural environments? How can these societies function in the metropolis? And even if the communes stand on explicitly anti-capitalist positions (both Enric Durán and Tarnac believe that the communes present autonomous systems outside the government and capitalism), is it really possible to live completely outside the system?

The first question is answered by Enric Durán. Admitting recently that the Catalan Integral Cooperative is not yet connected to other global commons, cooperatives and communes, Durán notes that the next logical step would be to integrate this local and regional work with the worldwide movement. The Invisible Committee's aim is inseparable from a direct confrontation with the system, enabled precisely by the political subjectivity created outside of it. But it also believes in the multiplication of communes, proliferating everywhere, in every factory, every school, every street, every village, every city, block by block, forming a network, a web of connections. In this sense, the commune is not only the basic unit of Partisan reality, of life in resistance, but the basic unit from which a more complex system can be built.

At the same time, the spreading of communes and their gradual interconnection eats away at the national myth: the collective fantasy of a homogeneous people which is 'Spanish' or 'French', 'Croatian' or 'Serbian'. It is precisely the experience of the communes that brings these young Spaniards and Frenchmen closer and divides them from the rest of the homogeneous Spanish or French society, calling into question the very model of national sovereignty. Whereas in the nation-state a certain class always draws on a common national identity in order to realize its shared interests, in the case of the communes it is the class struggle which enables the communards to go beyond the nation and its supposed common identity (Spanish, French and so on). It is here that something like a real collective identity can be formed. Whereas nationalist movements rely on the concept of the 'nation' as imagined community, sharing the same language, tradition and national history, anti-capitalist and anti-fascist movements deconstruct this idea of nationhood by building a community based on shared values and identities that go beyond the nation-state and national identities.[8]

So, yes, the experience of the commune can definitely be translated into different contexts: even unconnected, a commune can grow and develop itself in various localities. The task of universalizing the communes, going beyond the micro-local or local, is more difficult and complex, as it requires putting all these various communes – by definition decentralized autonomous systems – into a common framework of interconnections.

When it comes to the last – or more precisely, first and crucial – question, of whether it is really possible to live completely outside global capitalism, the existing communes and their accompanying theories reach their limits.

Let's imagine that we built a self-sustained and completely autonomous commune on a remote Croatian island with an existing population of ten people. Not in the countryside of Catalonia or in the inaccessible mountains of France, but even more remote from civilization, with a perfect climate for growing vegetables, farming and fishing. Let's imagine that, like Som Comunitat or Tarnac, this commune has developed not only an alternative economy with crypto-currencies and tools that successfully abolish private profits and private incomes, but a new society and value system based on equality and mutual respect. Let's imagine that this commune managed to become part of a bigger interconnected framework of other cooperatives and communes across Europe and beyond, enabling further development and greater autonomy (solar energy and water systems; free software and alternative internet, etc.).

Now let's imagine that this really existing island (unnamed, as hordes of tourists would instantly flock there) has a gorgeous blue cave which attracts thousands of tourists daily. The seas are swarming with speedboats chasing around the island; drones are an increasingly regular feature in the skies over its valleys and hills; Uber-boats (first inaugurated in summer 2017 in Croatia) and 'yacht weeks' descend upon the island several times a week. Once fish-filled seas are choked with plastic bottles and rubbish. How to survive on this island, even with the most sophisticated self-sustaining commune?

And let's imagine that suddenly, because other islands such as Lampedusa (Italy) or Lesbos (Greece) are already overcrowded, our island becomes the main hub for refugees fleeing new wars or the effects of climate change. We, the communards, help the drowning migrants, providing them with food, water and shelter. But since the EU signed a deal with Turkey to deport all refugees back to Turkey, the authorities not only start deporting them but threaten to evict our commune, as it doesn't follow European law.

There are no islands any more.

8

Mamma Mia! There Are No Islands Any More

'Alas,' said the mouse, 'the whole world is growing smaller every day. At the beginning it was so big that I was afraid, I kept running and running and I was glad when I saw walls far away to the right and left, but these long walls have narrowed so quickly that I am in the last chamber already, and there in the corner stands the trap that I must run into.'

'You only need to change your direction,' said the cat, and ate it up.[1]

Sounds familiar? It should.

Our world today resembles Franz Kafka's famous 'Little Fable'. Wherever we turn, it seems there is a trap waiting. A change in direction simply means ending up in a different trap.

Even if you decide to move to a remote island in the middle of the Adriatic Sea, 'civilization' – or the apocalypse – will surely reach you. When it does, it might be accompanied by the sounds of ABBA.

This is exactly what happened to me at the end of summer 2017 on Vis, when the producers of the Hollywood musical *Mamma Mia!* decided to shoot its sequel on the island where once 'the first sound from liberated Europe' was recorded.

Earlier that summer, rumours started to spread that, out of all the islands in the Mediterranean, Vis had been picked to play the imaginary Greek island of Kalokairi. After the news was confirmed, an advert went up on the *riva*, the waterfront, inviting people to become extras in the movie, asking women to come along with 'loose hair and with minimal make-up'. Since Vis was being turned into a Greek island, the locals were obviously supposed to play Greeks. They didn't much mind pretending for a few weeks: it was a quick way to earn some cash at the end of the summer season. But soon things started to change.

Even before the filming began that September, the undertaking – the most expensive foreign production in Croatia's history – drew intense media interest, which soon became global. British newspapers speculated that Vis could turn from a relatively unknown island into a tourist mecca. *The Times* of London published an article naming Croatia the film-makers' 'location of choice', with *Game of Thrones*, *Star Wars* and now *Mamma Mia! Here We Go Again* being shot there. The piece was accompanied by statements from salivating real estate agents, who boasted that every house, even if a ruin, on Vis flew off the market in a matter of days, most bought by well-off Brits and Norwegians.[2]

All of this was visible on the *riva* wall where the *Mamma Mia!* casting poster had gone up some days before. Instead of displaying the usual community and public notices, the wall was plastered with adverts from estate agencies and short messages saying: 'Buying anything on the island? Please call me.'

To see what might lie in store for Vis, it is worth looking at the fate of the Greek island of Skopelos, location of the first *Mamma Mia!* movie, which became the highest-grossing film and the fastest-selling DVD of all time in Britain. Tourists from all over the world invaded Skopelos. Hotels were booked up months in advance, bars and restaurants were packed and beaches were heaving with ABBA fans. Hourly ferries disgorged more of them, often in full song. The minuscule church on the hill that was featured in the musical (with a false front on its chapel) now attracts thousands of tourists who want to get married *Mamma Mia!*-style (it means converting to Greek Orthodoxy – which some do for the occasion). For locals, the island has turned into a nightmare. Property coming onto the market is quickly snapped up by investors, and the prices have skyrocketed – not just in real estate, but across the board. People are priced out of living on their own island.

Vis is now going through just such a transformation: you might call it a 'tourist occupation'.[3] In a world in which a single Hollywood musical can radically transform the life of a local community, for better or worse, there is obviously no escape, no outside. There are no more islands.

And so we return once again to the island where the 'first sound from occupied Europe' was recorded.

In his notorious so-called 'peace speech' of October 1939, Adolf Hitler announced his intention to impose a new order in Europe, an order based not on the idea of the nation-state but, ominously, 'a concept determined by blood': a racist, ethnically homogeneous new order with an agrarian 'Garden of Eden' in the East, which would serve as a reservoir of both raw materials and people. In this quest to spread the *Lebensraum* ('living space') of the German *Volk*, Hitler proclaimed, 'Today there are no longer any islands.' Soon, this new order would become one of the most ghastly self-fulfilling prophecies in history.[4]

In the course of realizing his plan, Hitler occupied nearly all the islands of the Adriatic, from Hvar to Brač, from Korčula to Mljet; only Vis was never occupied by the Nazis after the capitulation of fascist Italy in 1943.

One reason for this was the courageous Partisan resistance, which succeeded not only in liberating Vis from the fascists and defending it from Nazi occupation but also in liberating the other Nazi-occupied islands, and subsequently achieved the liberation of Belgrade and other parts of the mainland that would become the Federative Socialist Republic of Yugoslavia.

The other reason was the Partisan conviction that there can't be a 'free island' if other islands remain occupied. This brings us directly to our own responsibilities today and to the importance of building a global liberation movement before it is too late.

From the outside, from a distant European standpoint, the Partisan liberation struggle was regarded – if it was thought of at all – as a local business with little relevance for the wider international struggle that was taking place. Yet in 1943 and 1944 some 300,000 Partisans defied more than 850,000 occupying troops. The Nazis' intention was to destroy the Partisans, literally to 'throw them into the sea', which is one of the reasons why Yugoslav leader Josip Broz Tito, after several years of heavy guerrilla fighting throughout the mainland, established his headquarters on the remote island of Vis in 1944 (even today you can find a cave on the island called 'Tito's cave').

And it is during this period that the island of Vis acquired a historical and decisive role on the world stage. It was documented by the Scottish diplomat and adventurer Fitzroy Maclean – widely believed to have been the inspiration for Ian Fleming's James Bond – who parachuted into Yugoslavia in September 1943 as Winston Churchill's special envoy to Marshal Tito. Maclean spent an extraordinary eighteen months with the Partisans, from the mountains of Bosnia, through Vis, to the liberation of Belgrade in October 1944.

In his memoir *Eastern Approaches*, Fitzroy Maclean openly admits that he knew little about the Yugoslav situation before he was given his mission. The only news of Yugoslavia at that time concerned the activities of General Draža Mihajlović, holed up in the mountains with his Chetniks, whom the Allies, together with the royal government in exile, supported in the early days. Over time, information reached the British government from a variety of sources that the Chetniks were in fact collaborating with the enemy, and that the true resistance was by the armed bands bearing the name Partisans, led by a shadowy figure known as Tito. Hence, Maclean's mission. As he recounts, theories abounded as to Tito's true identity. One school of thought refused to believe that he existed at all. The name, they said, stood not for any individual leader but for an abbreviation: *Tajna Internacionalna Teroristička Organizacija* (T.I.T.O.), or Secret International Terrorist Organization. Another theory was that the leader's identity changed regularly, with a new 'Tito' nominated at frequent intervals. Others claimed that Tito was not a man but a young woman – not an impossibility given the number of female Partisans.

But what truly worried the British was not so much Tito's identity as that the Partisans were under communist leadership, with their ultimate aim being to establish in Yugoslavia a communist regime closely linked to Moscow. The first assumption was proven to be correct. The second, however, was increasingly called into question by the Partisans themselves, who were desperately waiting for Soviet help. Since Tito decided to lead the Partisan resistance as a national liberation movement independently of the directives of the Comintern, that help arrived only shortly before the liberation of Belgrade, at which point Tito made it clear to Stalin that it would be the Partisans, not the approaching Red Army, who would liberate Belgrade.

In *Eastern Approaches*, Fitzroy Maclean recalls a conversation with Winston Churchill at the prime minister's country residence of Chequers, while he prepared to parachute into Yugoslavia. Maclean asked Churchill bluntly: 'How would His Majesty's Government view such an eventuality' (a communist regime linked to Moscow in the heart of Europe)?[5]

'So long,' said Churchill, 'as the whole of Western civilization was threatened by the Nazi menace, we could not afford to let our attention be diverted from the immediate issue by considerations of long-term policy.' What Churchill meant, said Maclean, was that he 'was simply to find out who was killing the most Germans and suggest means by which we could help them to kill more. Politics must be a secondary consideration.'

So the real 'James Bond' of the twentieth century – if there ever was one – who had already spent two and a half years in the Soviet Union during Stalin's purges and who had fought in North Africa and the Middle East, finally parachuted into occupied Europe. The opening lines of Maclean's chapter 'Inside Europe' from *Eastern Approaches* is more dramatic than any James Bond novel:

> With a jerk my parachute opened and I found myself dangling, as it were at the end of a string, high above a silent mountain valley, greenish-grey and misty in the light of the moon . . . Somewhere above me the aircraft, having completed its mission, was headed for home. The noise of its engines grew gradually fainter in the distance. A long way below me and some distance away I could see a number of fires burning. I hoped they were the right ones, for the Germans also lit fires at night at different points in the Balkans in the hope of diverting supplies and parachutists from their proper destinations. As I swung lower, I could hear a faint noise of shouting coming from the direction of the fires. I could still not see the ground immediately beneath me. We must, I reflected, have been dropped from a considerable height to take so long in coming down. Then, without further warning, there was a jolt and I was lying in a field of wet grass. There was no one in sight. I released myself from the harness, rolled my parachute into a bundle, and set out to look for the Partisans.[6]

After landing in a secluded valley in the Bosnian mountains, Maclean soon reached Tito himself, and set in motion one of the greatest diplomatic and geostrategic achievements of the twentieth century. In Moscow, Maclean experienced the Soviet Revolution twenty years after the event; now he was in the middle of a struggle in its initial stages, with Yugoslav revolutionaries fighting for life and liberty against tremendous odds.

The Partisans had by then been fighting alone and unaided for two years against an overwhelming enemy. So when Maclean finally met Tito, the first question he was asked was, naturally: when were the Allies going to send the Partisans some arms?

In the garden of a ruined castle in the Bosnian town of Jajce, which housed the Partisans' headquarters, Tito and Fitzroy Maclean had conversations which no fiction writer, not even Ian Fleming, could have invented. Maclean's reply to Tito's demand for aid was straight-forward: he was, he said, a 'conservative', while Tito was a 'communist'. Then he asked Tito openly whether it was his ultimate aim to establish a communist state in Yugoslavia. Tito answered yes, but that it might have to be a gradual process. For the moment, the liberation move-ment was based politically on a popular front and not on a strictly one-party system. At the same time, the old order, with its political and economic institutions, was rapidly disintegrating due to occupa-tion and war, so when the dust settled very little would be left, and the way would be clear for a new system.

Maclean posed the crucial question: 'And will your new Yugo-slavia be an independent State or part of the Soviet Union?'

After a long pause, Tito replied. Maclean, he said, had to remem-ber the sacrifices which the Partisans were making in their struggle for independence, the hundreds of thousands of Yugoslavs – men, women and children – who had suffered torture and death. As to the Allies' fears about Yugoslavia becoming a satellite of Stalin's Soviet Union, he added, 'you need not suppose that we lightly cast aside a prize which has been won at such cost'.[7]

An experienced diplomat and politician, Maclean didn't take Tito's words at face value, but stayed with the Partisans to assess the situation on the ground. He was impressed by their discipline and dedication and their central organization and successful strategy of guerrilla war. And, as he began to form an idea of the extent and nature of the Partisan movement in Yugoslavia, he realized that here 'was something far more important both militarily and politically than anyone outside Yugoslavia suspected'.[8] What impressed him wasn't only their fight against all odds, but how they gave the character of revolution to what had started as a war. It was, Maclean felt, something unique in the whole of occupied Europe.

Accompanying the Partisans in their battles, living with and befriending many of the top cadres of future Yugoslavia (Vladimir Velebit, Edvard Kardelj, Moša Pijade, Koča Popović, among others), Maclean realized how wrong the British government was in supporting the Chetniks. In sending supplies and arms to the Chetniks, it had ended up helping the Nazis – since the Chetniks were using those same arms to fight the Partisans, who were in fact the only effective resistance to the Nazis. At the same time, Maclean became convinced that the Partisan war strategy was the only effective one.

As a result of Maclean's reports and after discussing Yugoslavia with Stalin and Roosevelt at the Tehran conference of November 1943, Churchill decided to switch British support to the Partisans. Shortly after, Maclean and Churchill met in Egypt.

During their historic conversation in Cairo, Fitzroy Maclean emphasized to Churchill that in his view the Partisans, whether they helped them or not, would become the decisive factor in Yugoslavia and, secondly, that Tito and the other leaders of the movement were openly and avowedly communist and that the system which they would establish would inevitably be on Soviet lines. Churchill replied: 'Do you intend to make Yugoslavia your home after the war?' 'No, Sir,' replied Maclean. 'Neither do I,' Churchill said, 'and, that being so, the less you and I worry about the form of Government they set up, the better. That is for them to decide. What interests us is, which of them is doing the most harm to the Germans.'[9]

Obviously the decision to back the Partisans didn't stem from the sudden conversion of Fitzroy Maclean and Winston Churchill into supporters of communism. Rather, it reveals a situation in which the Allied advance in Italy was still bogged down south of Rome and the Normandy landings were only a remote prospect, while the Germans still stood at the gates of Leningrad and Moscow and the Japanese remained undefeated. The Allies could not afford to neglect any potential ally, even if communist. Although Maclean and Churchill were fervent anti-communists, they knew that only by supporting the Partisans could they liberate occupied Europe. At this decisive moment they realized that there were no islands any more: that there was no local struggle that was not already part of the bigger geopolitical puzzle.

And isn't this one of the most important political and geopolitical lessons for our contemporary times? While Churchill was wise enough to support the Partisans, what we can see all over Europe – and the world – today is the establishment once again falling into the trap of supporting the wrong allies (as they did with the Chetniks), thereby fuelling right-wing extremism and populism and leading down a dangerous path. Today, many European countries are occupied by authoritarian and far-right regimes (Hungary, Poland, Austria, the Czech Republic), while in others the right is resurgent (France with Le Pen, Germany with Alternativ für Deutschland), and, last but not least, a permanent state of exception exists, from Paris to Hamburg.

Why do the 'leaders of the free world' not realize that by pushing more neoliberal reforms they are bringing about a situation in which the impoverished populations are, just like in the 1930s, turning increasingly towards the populist right?

What Maclean's extraordinary story teaches us is that the world of today could – if the Allies had not taken the decision to support the Partisans – look completely different: maybe, in fact, like the parallel reality of *The Man in the High Castle* in which the Nazis and the Japanese won the Second World War. If we don't want to end up in another 1940s, we must do the equivalent of supporting the Partisans today.

When today, so many decades after the historic period of 1944, *Mamma Mia!* is turning some of these sites of resistance into imaginary Greek tourist-movie attractions, when the local fishermen's language (a *lingua franca* spoken for more than 2,000 years) is dying out, when the only economy left is tourism, then we can see bluntly that there is no outside of global capitalism, there are no islands. Even a paradise can be quickly turned into a film set. Where once there was a sustainable local community, there are weekending EasyJet tourists, where fishermen's boats once rode at anchor, now luxury yachts are moored.

The lesson resides in the following: a local struggle can succeed only if it is a global struggle at the same time, and the global struggle can succeed only if it is grounded in the local. At a decisive moment, these local and global struggles became inseparable from each other, so that only by their unique relation, or the mutual reinforcement of the (temporary) alliance, the future of liberated Europe could be born.

What we must aim to create today are not just significant temporary alliances, but a truly international (between nations) – or, better, *transnational* (beyond nations) – liberation movement that might work both on the local and the global levels, by enacting a sort of dialectics between horizontality and verticality. But since such a movement has not yet come about, let us consider why we need this radical transnationalism to get us out of the current deadlock in the first place.

9

For a Global Liberation Movement

There is a beautiful scene in Costa-Gavras's 2012 movie *Capital* that starkly illustrates why we need a global transnational movement.

At a family dinner, the CEO of a giant European investment bank gets into a quarrel with his uncle, a '68 leftist, who accuses his nephew of indebting Europeans and destroying countries such as Greece.

The young banker answers: 'But you should be glad.'

Taken aback, the uncle asks: 'Why?'

'Because I'm fulfilling your childhood dreams,' says the nephew arrogantly.

'My childhood dreams?' questions the uncle, even more surprised.

'You lefties wanted internationalism, we've got it. Money knows no borders,' concludes the banker.

What this dialogue pinpoints is the crucial problem of today's globalism. It is not the internationalism of '68. This, the first truly global postwar uprising, ranged and raged from the United States, France, Germany, Poland, Italy to Vietnam, Brazil, Mexico. It radically transformed value systems and economic and social relations – but it didn't succeed in radically transforming the world. In fact, it was the increased financialization and rise of neoliberalism and the free-market doctrines of the 'Chicago School' that, in the years after '68, succeeded in imposing its own version of internationalism, the internationalism of capital.

And doesn't the same hold true for the last worldwide uprising, which occurred in 2011, from Occupy Wall Street to Tahrir Square, from Hong Kong to Sarajevo, from Puerta del Sol to Syntagma Square? Instead of radically transforming the global order which led to the great financial crash of 2007–8, these movements didn't succeed in creating a powerful international, or transnational, resistance movement – at least not yet. On the contrary, it is global capitalism and financialization (with its financial institutions, the stock market and multinational corporations), together with Silicon Valley's 'digital colonialism'* (from Facebook to Google), which is truly internationalist and global.

Yet even if they didn't become truly international, these struggles had characteristics, aims and objectives in common. They all point in the same direction – even if most of them were not fully aware of it. Or to put it in Hegel's terms, the movements of 2011 were internationalist *an sich* ('in themselves'): that's to say, their internationalism was implicit, potential, but they hadn't yet become explicitly internationalist – internationalist *für sich* ('for themselves'). The question, then, is how to move from *an sich* to *für sich*, how to realize this latent potential?

The first step is self-consciousness. This isn't simply about acknowledging that the most serious disasters humanity faces today – climate change and the threat of world war – are global problems which demand a global response. It is to realize that existing movements must become integrated into one single global resistance and liberation movement. Communes in France and Catalonia; 'rebel cities' such as Barcelona and Naples, which are not only fighting against Airbnb or Uber, but redefining what the very concept of national sovereignty means (when mayors across the south of Italy have admitted refugee boats in defiance of the government's prohibition);[1] crypto-currencies and alternative economies; occupations of theatres in Berlin (*Volksbühne*) and Rome (*Teatro Valle*); protests against the G20 in Hamburg and against the alt-right across the United States; whistleblowers from Edward Snowden to Julian Assange and digital activists; grassroots and indigenous movements across the world must join together as one.

One attempt to create something like a counter-hegemonic globalization was the World Social Forum (WSF), with its famous slogan 'Another world is possible'. During the most successful decade of the WSF – from its inauguration in Porto Alegre in 2001 until 2011 – it was the most relevant annual global activist meeting in the world. But

---

* I owe this term to Renata Avila, who is developing a theory of 'digital colonialism'

constant logistical problems, a tendency towards NGO-ization (instead of grassroots movements, the majority of participants of the later WSF were non-governmental organizations; the slow bureaucratization of the WSF itself) and internal ideological disagreements have impeded the Forum's ability to establish itself as a relevant political force with the power to influence global issues directly. It's no coincidence that the WSF's decade of success petered out in 2011, since it was in that year that the new political movements, from Occupy Wall Street to the Greek Spring, took the initiative of going a step further than the WSF in creating a global resistance movement and even taking power in some countries (such as Syriza in Greece).

To put it in more theoretical terms, the WSF was too horizontal (lots of debating and alliance-building) without the necessary verticality (more effective decision-making and organizational structures) to impose the WSF as a global political subject capable not only of tackling power on the national or international level, but also capable of tackling humanity's most pressing problems. Ultimately, it was this lack of leadership – that is, of political organization, including effective decision-making and self-management – that led to the WSF's decline and its growing irrelevance in the world after the 2011 uprisings.

Thanks to technology, personal friendships and shared struggles, today's movements are already more or less connected, but there is an absence of leadership at the transnational level, a lack of the kind of decision-making needed to transform this connectedness into a coordinated global resistance and liberation struggle. How can horizontality and verticality effectively be combined? How can a protest movement in Egypt or Guatemala reinforce a movement in Greece or Croatia, and vice versa?

Take something as complex as the current refugee crisis. If there ever was something that goes beyond national boundaries then it is this: the biggest displacement of people since the Second World War, according to the most recent annual figures of the UN refugee agency UNHCR, which records that around 68.5 million people are currently fleeing war or persecution worldwide.[2] Responses at the horizontal – municipal or even national – level, such as solidarity and anti-war movements, are obviously crucial, but in themselves can never address the root causes of this problem. Long-term geo-political, social and economic solutions can be achieved only by a mutually interconnected movement with a leadership structure at all levels: local, national, international.

A useful historical example of how struggles have to be coordinated and connected on all levels is an almost forgotten story of Yugoslav refugees who, fleeing the Nazis in 1944, passed through the island of Vis en route to refugee camps in Egypt.

That year, fearing massive reprisals by the German army, the region of Dalmatia was evacuated and more than 37,000 refugees – many of whom had been living in forests and caves for years – arrived on Vis. At the beginning of January 1944, the island's population stood at 24,000, of which 8,000 were permanent inhabitants; over 10,000 were refugees, mostly women and children. Since all the refugees couldn't be taken into the British-controlled Italian city of Bari, with fighting still raging between the Allies and the retreating German army, the Yugoslav refugees were transferred to Egypt to three camps on the edge of the Sinai Desert. There they lived under canvas, worked and struggled in the baking sands for some eighteen months, from summer 1944 to the beginning of 1946. One of these camps, around 260 square kilometres in size, was El Shatt. Its story carries an important lesson for us today.

Although under British and US protection, the refugees were largely left to fend for themselves. The day following their arrival at the camp, a group of English officers, expecting to find a mass of helpless refugees, were surprised to see the first issue of *Naš list* ('Our Paper'), the newspaper of the refugees' central committee.

Right from the start the new arrivals began to organize themselves and develop forms of self-management. They divided El Shatt into five sub-camps, each set up roughly along the lines of a small Yugoslav village. Soon, the administration of the camp was almost completely controlled by the refugees. They established their own courts and even police force, they started kindergartens, elementary schools, secondary schools, nursing schools, trade schools and published a newspaper. The camp had its own theatre, recreation hall, store houses, repair shops, infirmary, laundry and so on.

Today, as millions flee Africa for Europe, the wartime refugees of

Yugoslavia who founded a new society in the Sinai Desert teach us something significant about the relation between horizontality and verticality. Not only was El Shatt one of the first camps managed by refugees themselves, it was probably the first successful Yugoslav experience of self-management, later to become the main economic model of the new Yugoslavia.

If on the one hand we can find a vertical leadership in the Partisan movement, a movement simultaneously connected to the international struggle against Nazism and fascism, we also find horizontality in the localized construction of a new society. The message here is clear. We already have to be the very society that we are aiming to build. There is no 'day after' when the new society will be built. It must be built even before it can exist; it has to exist before it can be built. This is what we could call the 'concrete universality' of true resistance.

If we understand El Shatt as the horizontality and the Partisan movement on the other side of the Adriatic as verticality, then it is only by a sort of dialectics, in which the horizontal and the vertical are mutually reinforcing, that liberation can take place: a liberation which is always in a state of becoming. And this is the precondition for any successful global resistance and liberation movement. The horizontal and vertical, the local and the global, must go hand in hand. In today's context, it shows how a complex organization might be born out of the recomposition and reconnection of the experiences of all forms of activism around the world.

Another useful historical example of how effective resistance must combine the horizontal and the vertical is the Non-Aligned Movement. Its origins lie in the Bandung Conference of 1955 when, as the Cold War intensified, the Indonesian president Sukarno brought together leaders from Yugoslavia's Tito, India's Nehru and Indira Gandhi, to Egypt's Nasser, the Democratic Republic of Vietnam's Ho Chi Minh and China's Zhou Enlai. Instead of joining either the blocs of the USA or Soviet Union, they agreed to remain neutral, to create a third bloc. The following year the Non-Aligned Movement was founded on the then Yugoslav island of Brijuni – on the same Adriatic coast as Vis.

The five principles on which the Non-Aligned Movement is based are:

1. Mutual respect for each other's territorial integrity and sovereignty
2. Mutual non-aggression
3. Mutual non-interference in domestic affairs
4. Equality and mutual benefit
5. Peaceful coexistence

As always, when we are faced with a set of principles, there is room for scepticism. Usually, once a movement or institution declares its principles, it begins breaking – or at least diluting – them. Take Cuba, which, though technically non-aligned, allied itself with the Soviets during the Cold War, or India's alliance with the Soviets in their fight against China. A decisive moment for the future of the Non-Aligned Movement came in 1979 during the Soviet invasion of Afghanistan, an act of aggression that split the movement down the middle: one half supporting it, the other half opposing it. At that year's meeting of the movement in Havana, the Jamaican prime minister Michael Manley briefly mentioned this rupture, while at the same time proposing an alliance between the Non-Aligned Movement and the Soviet Union to battle imperialism. 'We may call ourselves communists, socialists or humanists or simply progressive,' he stated, 'but all [are] anti-imperialists.'

With the end of the Cold War, and especially after the breakup of its historical founding member Yugoslavia, the movement, already in decline, lost its *raison d'être*. Although an astonishing number of countries – 120 – had joined it, it didn't have the necessary impetus to redefine itself and reinvent its purpose in the changing world system. As with the decline of the World Social Forum – a transnational movement not formed of states, but movements – the main problem was the size of the organization and the diversity of agendas and political interests among its members. Although the movement staggered on, there was an astonishing absence of substantial action on any of the international issues in the last decades. By the time Venezuela hosted the seventeenth summit of the Non-Aligned Movement in September 2016, its irrelevance had become clear. Back in 2012 some thirty-five heads of state had attended the previous summit in Tehran; only ten attended in 2016. The current positions of the Non-Aligned

Movement – criticism of US foreign policy, support for sustainable development, cooperation among the countries of the Global South – might be attributed to any modern progressive groups, from the various Occupy movements to progressive parts of the US Democrats advocating a Green New Deal to the British Labour Party. And these have done more of substance in the last few decades than the whole Non-Aligned Movement combined. One of the reasons lies in the fact that it consists of states and not movements. Namely, that its organizational structure is already conditioned by the interests of the ruling classes of different states which, after the end of the Cold War, were not even united on the basic principles of non-alignment.

The Non-Aligned Movement's failure is crucial for us today. The 1989 fall of the Berlin Wall brought to an end the coexistence of three systems: Western social-democracy (Germany, France, United States), communism (Soviet Russia) and the non-aligned states. Today, with the world subordinated to capital, what we need is a rebooted non-aligned movement, one refocused on the struggle against all forms of occupation and domination by capital. But this renewed non-aligned movement, unlike the historical and nominally existing one, should not consist only of governments (there are not that many progressive governments yet). It would embrace movements operating horizontally, from alternative markets in Greece to various occupations of theatres, cinemas and squares, and also existing progressive political parties and municipalist movements. And it would not simply be aligned with major power blocs or nation-states. It would, first and foremost, be aligned against major power blocs of capital which know no borders. What it would be aligned against is global capitalism itself.

This is why, unlike the original Non-Aligned Movement, whose members were particularly concentrated in countries considered to be developing or part of the Global South, this new global resistance and liberation movement would need strong anchors (movements, trade unions, whistleblowers, political parties, governments) in the most developed capitalist countries (United States, Germany, but also Russia, China, South Korea and others). This new movement would not limit itself to annual meetings, networking and declarations. It would undertake concrete and coordinated local, national and transnational actions that would be able to tackle and solve the crucial threats to humanity – ecological disasters, migration, subjugation to capitalism and techno-totalitarianism.

There is a pressing need for a movement along these lines. The long response to the 2008 crisis wasn't simply to be found in the likes of Occupy Wall Street and Gezi Park, the Indignados or Black Lives Matter, Sanders and Corbyn. With the inevitable failure of the neo-liberal response to solve the internal contradictions of capitalism, we have over the last decade witnessed not only the rise of authoritarian capitalism (Erdoğan and Putin, Trump and Modi) but something arguably much more dangerous, perhaps best described by the British historian and activist Tariq Ali as the 'extreme centre'.[3]

What we are seeing today is not so much the rise of openly fascist political parties, but the transformation of the whole political landscape into an extreme centre, in which the 'Fascist International' (with its historical revisionism and xenophobia) and the 'Neoliberal International' (with its privatization of healthcare and education, increasing debt-based economy) reinforce each other. It is the failure of global neoliberalism to deal with the financial crash of 2007–8 which deepened that crisis, creating a fertile ground for the rising Fascist International. As the crash of the late 1920s led to the rise of fascism and Nazism, so the politics of Angela Merkel (both her stance towards refugees and her inability to solve the Eurozone crisis) has led to the rise of the German Alternative für Deutschland. It was the former French president Hollande's neoliberal response to the crisis of 2008 that led to Le Pen. And it is the Democrats themselves, with their neoliberal response to the crash and their favouring of Hillary Clinton over Bernie Sanders, who helped bring about Donald Trump.

In confronting the current situation, then, we must see past the false dilemma of the choice that we're constantly presented with, of capitalism or fascism (Hillary Clinton or Donald Trump, Merkel or Alternative für Deutschland, Macron or Le Pen). The truly radical response to our predicament can only reside in the creation of a 'third option', which would move beyond this choice between two sides of the same coin. We should remember an old Armenian joke popular in the Eastern bloc during the Cold War. A listener calls in to Radio Yerevan and asks: 'Which tea is better, Chinese or Soviet?'

The answer comes: 'Don't get mixed up in a confrontation between superpowers, drink coffee.'

This was the Non-Aligned Movement's philosophy in a nutshell. And the same holds true today: instead of the Kool Aid of Austerity International or Fascist International, as their confrontation brings us to the verge of a Third World War, or at the very least the endless prolongation of the current state of exception, we should be creating a global movement that can effectively oppose both. We should be creating the first truly global community.

10
Poetry from the Future

In creating a new global liberation movement – one that would work across borders and beyond national identities, which would go beyond the false dichotomy of the choice presented to us between neoliberalism and fascism – we have myriad inspiring examples, historical and contemporary, on which to draw. But if we want to build such a transnational liberation movement for our times, with a new name and new language, one that, while remembering the past also avoids its mistakes, then the inspiration has to come from the future.

This chronological paradox was best summed up by Karl Marx in the opening pages of his 1852 work *The Eighteenth Brumaire of Louis Bonaparte*. There, he contrasts the bourgeois revolutions of the eighteenth century and the proletarian revolutions of his own time:

> The social revolution of the nineteenth century cannot take its poetry from the past but only from the future. It cannot begin with itself before it has stripped away all superstition about the past. The former revolutions required recollections of past world history in order to smother their own content. The revolution of the nineteenth century must let the dead bury their dead in order to arrive at its own content. There the phrase went beyond the content – here the content goes beyond the phrase.[1]

What did Marx mean by 'poetry'? In fact, he wasn't talking about poetry as we commonly understand the term, but *poiesis*, from the ancient Greek verb *poiein*, which means 'to produce' in the sense of bringing something into being. In this sense, Marx himself had already invented the poetry of the future revolutions four years previously in his *Communist Manifesto*. And, as the French philosopher Étienne Balibar shows, Marx did something else as well.[2] He removed one of philosophy's most ancient taboos, namely, the radical distinction between *praxis* (from *prattein*, 'to do' in the sense of acting) and *poiesis* established by Aristotle. Marx's formulation is what Balibar calls a 'revolutionary thesis', because there is neither *praxis* nor *poiesis* any longer taking primacy over the other. Rather *praxis* constantly passes over into *poiesis* and vice versa. In other words, if the new social revolution has to draw its poetry from the future, the content of the future revolution can be made only out of the poetry which is at the same time *poiesis* and *praxis*. The action (*praxis*) has to bring into being (*poiesis*) something that is a new creation of life and society by the very acts which happen in the present and come from the future.

The problem with the poetry from the past is precisely this: it borrows from the past. Luther's Protestant revolution had referenced the apostle Paul; the French bourgeois revolution, Roman antiquity (the ideals of liberty, equality and fraternity); the Haitian revolution, the French Revolution; and last but not least many new left parties today draw inspiration from the social-democracy of the twentieth century (wealth redistribution, progressive taxation and so on), instead of offering something much more radical and responding to the future. Instead of breaking into the future with eyes turned to the past, a truly new social revolution must draw its content from the future. This is why, as Benjamin recalls in his 'Theses on the Philosophy of History', the people on the first evening of fighting in Paris in July 1789 were simultaneously and independently firing at clock towers across the city. The new revolution had – literally – to create its own time.

And it is here that we must return to Benjamin's notion of time:

A historical materialist cannot do without the notion of a present which is not a transition, but in which time stands still and has come to a stop. For this notion defines the present in which he himself is writing history. Historicism gives the 'eternal' image of the past; a historical materialist leaves it to others to be drained by the whore called 'Once upon a time' in historicism's bordello. He remains in control of his powers, man enough to blast open the continuum of history.[3]

While the members of the French Revolution were never contemporaries of their own actions, because they were breaking into the future in the 'costume' provided by past moments of emancipation (such as the Roman 'republican' or 'spartacist' phraseology, or citing the mythic Roman accomplishments of liberty, equality and fraternity),[4] the new revolutionaries have to inhabit the now of history, what Benjamin calls in his thesis XIV *die Jetztzeit* ('now-time' or 'here-and-now'). In order to draw our inspiration from the future, we must escape from the blandishments of the past: we must shoot the clocks of the present in order to break out into the future.

No wonder Benjamin uses the same example as Marx in his *Eighteenth Brumaire*, referring to the French Revolution as one that 'viewed itself as Rome reincarnate' and 'evoked ancient Rome the way fashion evokes costumes of the past'. While this sort of revolution was, as Benjamin beautifully describes it, 'a tiger's leap into the past' (because 'the jump takes place in an arena where the ruling class gives the commands'), the new revolution has to make a leap into 'the open air of history', imposing its own rules of the game. In this way, the *Jetztzeit* is time at a standstill, a kind of 'zero hour'.[5]

Today, as we witness a reincarnation of fascism in different costumes all over the world, we find ourselves in an analogous situation. We can't be breaking into the future with our eyes turned to the past, for the overwhelming reason that the solution to the world's problems doesn't lie in modest proposals for wealth redistribution, social democracy or traditional protests or party politics. This, of course, doesn't mean that we can't or shouldn't learn from the past. On the contrary, it is the past and its unfulfilled potentials which point towards the potentiality of the future.

But in order to make this crucial leap into 'the open air of history' we have to be acting and living in the now-time. It means breaking once and for all with the historicist notion of history understood as *kronos*: the purely linear and chronological vision of events usually perceived as a succession of dates in the columns of a calendar. What Benjamin teaches us, on the contrary, is an understanding of history as *kairos*: time as an open and unfinished process. It means – and here we come full circle – that the BBC recordings on Vis in 1944, the 'first sound from occupied Europe', might be understood not simply as a sound from the past, but as a sound from the future.

When a movement shatters or a comrade dies – someone with whom you were connected through struggle and conviction, going beyond mere friendship – nothing is lost so long as the struggle continues and conviction grows. Yet everything might be lost, if at that devastating moment we are not able to continue, even stronger, as if our comrades and their struggles were still with us. Even if they are not physically among us any more, to carry the spark of conviction and resistance into the future entails a chance of resurrection. The point is not just to remember, but to live as if the comrades and their struggles are here, in the now-time, to debate with them here and now, to quarrel if needed, to think and rethink, to have fun, to laugh and play and dream together, by deconstructing time itself and the prevailing notion that what has passed has passed for ever We have to understand the temporality of struggle as something which is not *kronos*, a mere succession of events (the Paris Commune, the French Revolution, the October Revolution, the anti-slavery movement, Occupy, the Greek Spring, Tahrir, the Partisans), but another space, another time, another reality which is not past but is here and now. The potentials of the past can only be re-activated by changing the present. And it is in this newly shaped present that the future can be created.

But 'Time is over!' We are constantly reminded not only that the utopias of the past century have disappeared, but that we live in an age without any big narratives – except that of 'there is no alternative', a negative narrative *par excellence*. Instead of inhabiting the now-time, we inhabit a vicious 'presentism', defined pithily by Enzo Traverso as a 'suspended time between an unmasterable past and a denied future, between a "past that won't go away" and a future that cannot be invented or predicted (except in terms of catastrophe)'.[6]

If 'Time is over', aren't we inevitably approaching a deadlock similar to Franz Kafka's 'Little Fable', or what Walter Benjamin would call *Einbahnstrasse*, a one-way street? If Jean-Jacques Rousseau could proclaim in the prophetic passage from his 1762 *Emile* that 'we are approaching the state of crisis and the century of revolutions', shouldn't we today accept that we live in an age in which the opposite seems to be the case: 'Not the imminent return of revolutions, but the exhaustion of the idea, or – which is not exactly the same – the accumulation of factors which make the failure of revolutions their only possible outcome, therefore depriving them of their historical meaning and their political effectivity'?[7]

In other words, if the future is cancelled, if time is literally over, how can we draw our inspiration from the poetry from the future? How can we read or write the poetry from the future?

The answer is simultaneously simple and complex: we can do it only in the present, only in the *now*. Yet this now can't be confused with the capitalist presentism in which either past or future no longer have any meaning; where 'fake news' and historical revisionism have already erased almost all distinctions between reality and fiction. It is this particular moment (*Jetztzeit*) in which the potentials of the past re-emerge (the first sound from occupied Europe, the Arab Spring and the Greek Spring, all the protests and occupations from Black Lives Matter to *Gilets jaunes* and so on) not as something *gewesene* ('what has been'), but as *kairos*, an open and unfinished project.

But here it comes again: 'Time is over!' We are reminded by the galloping steps of fascism (from the United States to Europe and beyond) and capitalist destruction (from the brutal extraction of natural and human resources to the realistic possibility of a nuclear war or ecological armageddon). And here again, the only seemingly paradoxical answer to the cancellation of the future is now. It is, as counterintuitive as it might seem at first glance, precisely the inevitable collapse of civilization which – today more than ever – makes revolution inevitable. If there is no revolution, it is surely the end of the world.

An obscure text by the French philosopher Maurice Blanchot, 'The apocalypse is disappointing', published in 1964, during the height of the Cold War, provides a surprising answer. The significance of Blanchot's text – similar to Kubrick's exactly contemporary *Dr Strangelove, or: How I Learned to Stop Worrying and Love the Bomb* – was recently rediscovered by the Slovenian philosopher Alenka Zupančič. Blanchot's main argument is that the threat of the 'Bomb' (the master signifier) and its potential of total annihilation led to the birth of the idea of a whole (of the world), as the whole, precisely, that can be lost, or disappear for ever.[8]

You might ask, why does this shed any light on our current crisis? Because without this sense of the whole, there is no way out. The apocalypse is disappointing in that there is no discernible whole, which is devoid of any concrete content and form. While people bond together in the face of a common threat (lethal hurricanes, wars, terrorist attacks, refugee crises, ecological disasters, or the total annihilation of humanity) there is not yet the sense of a *global community*. This very whole (totality) of which some of us born after the Bomb became aware for the first time at the beginning of the twenty-first century is about to disappear, but it is not yet a totality in the sense of a human community.

The ingenuity of Blanchot, says Zupančič, resides in the following Hegelian twist. Instead of accepting or denying the idea of the apocalypse, it is precisely its inevitability that lays the foundations for a predictable revolution (in the sense that only revolution can prevent the apocalypse, turning it from an unavoidable future event into something that is no longer inevitable). The global threats to humanity that we are now encountering represent an opportunity to build this coming global community. The apocalypse is disappointing because we will lose something (the whole) that we didn't succeed in building. But it is precisely by creating what we are about to lose that we could eventually prevent the end.

> What does the problematic event teach us? This: that insofar as it puts into question the human species in its totality, it is also because of this event that the idea of totality arises visibly and for the first time on our horizon – a sun, though we know not whether it is rising or setting; also, that this totality is in our possession, but as a negative power. This singularly confirms the preface to the *Phenomenology of Spirit*: the power of understanding is an absolute power of negation; understanding knows only through the force of separation, that is, of destruction – analysis, fission – and at the same time knows only the destructible and is certain only of what could be destroyed. Through understanding, we know very precisely what must be done in order for the final annihilation to occur, but we do not know which resources to solicit to prevent it from occurring. What understanding gives us is the knowledge of catastrophe, and what it predicts, foresees, and grasps, by means of decisive anticipation, is the possibility of the end. Thus

man is held to the whole first of all by the force of understanding, and understanding is held to the whole by negation. Whence insecurity of all knowledge – of knowledge that bears on the whole.[9]

What this Hegelian reading of the apocalypse enables us to become aware of is that *the future is now*. This is the dark future of disastrous hurricanes which leave whole islands and countries devastated, in response to which Trump throws paper towels into Puerto Rican crowds.[10] Yes, it is the totalitarian future in which people gather to demand their basic democratic rights, and are the victims of a brutal crackdown by the security services.

What if this dystopian future which is our daily present can give rise to a collective, global awareness about the whole: an awareness that might allow us to shape the future? What if the coming apocalypse opens up a *chance*, maybe for the first time (since the threat is not only the Bomb any more but a multiplicity of global threats), not only to understand humanity as *the whole*, as a totality, but to create a totality in the sense of a *global community* that would be structured in a radically different way from the one we are inhabiting now? And this 'avatar of totality', which necessarily comes *from* the future (*aus der Zukunft*),[11] is actually our only chance to avoid the apocalypse?

As paradoxical as it might sound, when the Caribbean was pummelled by destructive hurricanes in September 2017, this was our chance; when, that same month, Mexico was hit by a massive earthquake this was our chance; and when, halfway across the world, the people of Catalonia, demanding their democratic right to vote over independence, were slapped down by the police and special forces: this, too, was our chance. The same goes for all the fascist movements, walls and detention centres rising like mushrooms around the globe; for the Facebook–Cambridge Analytica revelations, for the war in Syria or in Yemen, for the refugee crisis, for the record heatwaves in Europe and microplastic-filled oceans. Each of these events represented an alarm call from a catastrophic future that is inevitable – inevitable only if we are not able to create a *global community* which would perceive and treat each of these tragic events (from Puerto Rico to Florida, from police brutality in Hamburg to Catalonia, from rising fascism in Budapest to Charlottesville) as part of a whole.

But, here again comes the devil's advocate with his alarming 'There is no time!', 'Everything is going to collapse if we don't act right now!' And this is exactly what we should be avoiding. We should always distinguish between the fake now and the now as *Jetztzeit*. If mere presentism (the fake now or the nowness of the fake) consists in the reproduction of the present by instant news, real-time politics, society of spectacle, then the *Jetztzeit*, the here-and-now, consists in a deconstruction and destruction of the temporal totalitarianism which imposes and enforces a notion of time that necessarily narrows possibilities and potentialities. To act now means to create the conditions for our own future, not to follow the already written script from the past: it means to produce a crack in the present, a disruption in the imposition of capitalist temporality, the rhythm of power.

This sort of temporal subversion is nicely encapsulated in an event that happened in May 1995 during the Zapatista negotiations with the Mexican government. The government officials put forth a proposal and demanded a quick response from the Zapatistas. The Zapatistas, however, replied that a response would take some time as they needed to consult with their communities: 'We as Indians, have rhythms, forms of understanding, of deciding, of reaching agreements.' The government negotiators started making fun of the Zapatistas. 'We don't understand why you say that because we see you have Japanese watches, so how do you say you are wearing indigenous watches, that's from Japan.' To which the Zapatistas said, 'You haven't learned. You understand us backwards. We use time, not the clock.'[12]

This is another enactment of Benjamin's struggle against *kronos* or, more precisely, a deconstruction of the notion of time as a set of chronological and linear events, a struggle against the most powerful of all powers (time). Of course, you could claim that the rapid technological and ontological acceleration of capitalism and its total colonization of time will inevitably affect also those, from Mexico's Zapatistas to the island of Vis and its philosophy of *pomalo*, who live on the fringes of capitalist temporality.

The Zapatistas have an answer to this as well. In April 2017 Subcomandante Galeano (formerly known as Subcomandante Marcos) delivered a lecture in San Cristobal de las Casas, a town in the southern Mexican state of Chiapas, entitled 'Prelude: Timepieces, the Apocalypse, and the Hour of the Small'. In contrast to the predominant capitalist concept of time according to which the Zapatistas and all other groups and societies that are not living in the capitalist temporality are usually perceived as 'anachronistic' (literally, in ancient Greek, 'against time'), 'backward' or 'lazy' (stereotypically the Greeks), Subcomandante Galeano compares the Zapatistas to the hourglass:

> An hourglass that, although it doesn't request an update every 15 minutes and doesn't require you to have credit on your phone to work, does have to renew its limited countdown over and over again. Although not very practical and somewhat uncomfortable, just like us Zapatistas, the hourglass has its advantages. For example, in it we can see the time that has gone by, the past, and try to understand it. And we can see, too, the time that is coming. Zapatista time cannot be understood without understanding the gaze that keeps track of time with an hourglass. That's why, on this one and only occasion, we've brought here for you, madam, sir, other, little girl, little boy, this hourglass which we've baptized the 'You know nothing, Jon Snow' model.[13]

It is difficult to not be affected by Subcomandante Galeano's subtle irony and his gentle way of translating something from Zapatista philosophy into our Western language through the culture of Hollywood. Here we have someone who has devoted his life to the fight against the capitalist colonization of time, but instead of taking refuge in anachronistic explanations, he uses a quote from *Game of Thrones*. He chose it with care: it comes from a scene of utter misunderstanding, in which the wildling girl Ygritte tells Jon Snow – who asked why she was crying because of a song about 'the last of the giants' when he had just seen hundreds of them – how little he knows about the real world.

Why did the Subcomandante call the hourglass the 'Jon Snow model'? The answer is that Zapatista time cannot be understood without understanding *the gaze* that keeps track of time with an hourglass. The Western, capitalist notion of time demands that we pay attention to that brief instant in which a tiny grain of sand arrives in the narrow passage, to fall and join the other moments that have accumulated in what we call the 'past'. This is the prevailing presentism which commands us to live in the moment: don't look back, because 'a second ago' is the same as 'a century ago' – and above all, don't look at what's coming.

In opposition to this prevailing presentism, the Zapatistas, as Sub-comandante Galeano says,

> ... stubbornly, against the grain, just to be contrary (without insulting anybody in particular, to each his own), are analyzing and questioning the tiny grain of sand that exists anonymously in the middle of all the others, waiting its turn to get in line in the narrow tunnel, and at the same time looking at the grains that lie below and to the left in what we call the 'past', asking each other what the heck they have to do with this presentation about the walls of Capital and the cracks below. And we have one eye on the cat and the other on the meat hook, or rather the dog, with which the 'cat-dog'* becomes a tool of analysis in critical thought and ceases to be the constant company of a little girl who imagines herself without fear, free, a *compañera*.[14]

What the subcomandante unfolds here is nothing less than a philosophy of struggle, in which Zapatismo – for the Zapatistas themselves – is one struggle among many, perhaps a small grain of sand that exists in the middle of all the others: it is the *poetry from the future* in which many worlds fit: all of them, those that existed, those that exist and those yet to be born. The struggle, says Sub-comandante Galeano, is something 'that requires you to pay attention to the whole and to the parts, and to be ready because that last grain of sand isn't the last, but rather, the first, and that the hourglass must be turned over because it contains not today, but yesterday, and yes, you're right, tomorrow too'.[15]

---

* To understand what the cryptic 'cat-dog' means (originally from the saying *'con un ojo en el gato y otro en el garabato'*, literally 'with one eye on the cat and the other on the meat hook', meaning to keep an eye on two things at once), we have to look at a script from the future, supposedly for a science fiction film, which was left by the late Subcomandante Marcos called 'Toward what does the gaze look'

In other words, the Zapatista understanding of time is that of *kairos*. It means that all our emancipatory struggles, the ones of the past and the ones to come, with all their differences and outcomes, have to be perceived as one and the same struggle. And even if some of these struggles, with all their dreams, hopes and achievements, might appear as nothing more than a tiny grain of sand in an hour-glass, we always have to remember that even this tiny grain of sand can at the same time already be a mountain. It just depends on the gaze. And from where we draw our poetry.

Notes

PROLOGUE: THE FIRST SOUND
FROM OCCUPIED EUROPE

1. See Ronald Hayman, *Writing Against: Biography of Sartre*, Little-hampton Book Services, 1986
2. The original recording can be found in the 'Papers of (William) Denis Johnston', at Trinity College, Dublin, which has a collection of Johnston's writings and recordings. See http://www.iar.ie/Archive.shtml?IE TCD MS/10066
3. One evening in early May 1975, when the recording was transmitted for the first time in thirty years, a radio lover, Majo Topolovac, heard it as he listened to Radio London. He and the Sarajevo journalist Zoran Udovičić worked for two years on its reconstruction and also searched for new documents. They recorded hundreds of hours across Yugoslavia, looking for witnesses to the event in order to prove where the recording took place. The result of their investigation was a documentary radio-drama called *These people know what they are fighting for*, about sixty minutes long, with two layers that constantly overlap: the original recording from 1944 and the reconstruction of voices and atmosphere during their investigation. See: Zoran Udovičić and Majo Topolovac, '*S one strane Jadrana: tragom prvog zvučnog dokumenta u okupiranoj*' ('On the other side of the Adriatic: Following the trail of the first sound picture from Occupied Europe'), *Europi*, Sarajevo, Media Plan Institut, 2003. The reconstruction of the original BBC recording can be found here: https://soundcloud.com/mediacentarsa rajevo/dokumentarna-radio-reporta-a-s
4. Ibid.
5. Walter Benjamin, *Illuminations: Essays and Reflections*, ed. Hannah Arendt, trans. Henry Zohn, 1968; Schocken Books, 2007, p. 255

6. Ibid.

7. See Srećko Horvat and Igor Štiks (eds.), *Welcome to the Desert of Post-Socialism: Radical Politics After Yugoslavia*, Verso, 2014

8. This chapter is based on the best historical account of the resistance and liberation movement on the island of Vis between 1941 and 1945: Veseljko Huljić, *Vis 1941–1945*, Institut za historiju radničkog pokreta Dalmacije, 1979

9. Ibid.

10. Among the many accounts of the Yugoslav resistance and liberation movement, besides Fitzroy Maclean's seminal *Eastern Approaches*, helpful to get a view from the 'outside' not only on its historical relevance but also on the island of Vis itself are the following books: Fitzroy Maclean, *The Heretic: The Life and Times of Josip Broz Tito*; William Deakin, *Embattled Mountain*; Bill Strutton, *Island of Terrible Friends*; Sterling Hayden, *Wanderer*; and Winston Churchill, *Second World War*. As always, one of the best accounts was written by the intelligence services, in this case the OSS Report on a visit to the Yugoslav National Army of Liberation in 1943

11. The original recording can be found in the 'Papers of (William) Denis Johnston', at Trinity College, Dublin. A reconstruction of the original BBC recording can be found here: https://soundcloud.com/mediacentarsarajevo/dokumentarna-radio-reporta-a-s

12. Ibid.

I. SUMMER IN HAMBURG: BACK TO THE FUTURE

1. 'Hamburg is transforming itself into an Orwellian dystopia for the G20 summit', DiEM25: https://diem25.org/hamburg-is-transforming-itself-into-an-orwellian-dystopia-for-the-g20-summit/

2. 'Ghost town: how China emptied Hangzhou to guarantee "perfect" G20', *Guardian*, 5 September 2016: https://www.theguardian.com/world/2016/sep/05/ghost-town-how-china-emptied-hangzhou-to-guarantee-perfect-g20

3. 'Panda diplomacy: Merkel and Xi pushed into awkward embrace before G20', Reuters, 4 July 2017: https://www.reuters.com/article/us-g20-germany-china/panda-diplomacy-merkel-and-xi-pushed-into-awkward-embrace-before-g20-idUSKBN19P16G

4. 'US-Saudi Arabia seal weapons deal worth nearly $110 billion . . .', CNBC, 20 May 2017: https://www.cnbc.com/2017/05/20/us-saudi-

arabia-seal-weapons-deal-worth-nearly-110-billion-as-trump-begins-
visit.html

5. https://www.businessinsider.com/top-countries-exporting-weapons-
arms-sales-2018-3

6. 'Beethoven's Ninth at the G20: Peace, joy – and provocation', Deutsche
Welle, 7 July 2017: http://www.dw.com/en/beethovens-ninth-at-the-
g20-peace-joy-and-provocation/a-39594778

7. 'Turkey: Erdoğan threatens to "clean" Gezi Park of "terrorists"', 13
June 2013: https://www.theguardian.com/world/middle-east-live/2013/
jun/13/turkey-referendum-plan-mooted-as-erdo-an-sets-protesters-dead
line-live-coverage

8. 'France: Unchecked clampdown on protests under guise of fighting terrorism', Amnesty International, 31 May 2017: https://www.amnesty.
org/en/latest/news/2017/05/france-unchecked-clampdown-on-protests-
under-guise-of-fighting-terrorism/

9. See Giorgio Agamben, *The State of Exception*, University of Chicago
Press Books, 2005

10. 'Linker Hass kaum zu stoppen. Die Guerilla-Taktik der G20', *Bild*,
8 July 2017

11. 'German foreign minister: G20 rioters no different from "neo-Nazis"',
Politico, 9 July 2017: http://www.politico.eu/article/german-foreign-
minister-g20-rioters-no-different-from-neo-nazis/

12. 'Rare bipartisan unity in Germany on post-Hamburg extremist database', *Politico*, 10 July 2017: http://www.politico.eu/article/rare-
bipartisan-unity-in-germany-on-post-hamburg-extremist-database-g20/

13. Owen Jones, 'If my sister can be drawn into the anti-terror net,
imagine the risk to others', *Guardian*, 26 October 2017: https://www.
theguardian.com/commentisfree/2017/oct/26/schedule-7-terrorism-act-
2000-activism-civil-rights-ethnic-minorities

14. See Michel Foucault, 'Of Other Spaces: Utopias and Heterotopias'
(lecture given in March 1967), available in English: http://web.mit.
edu/allanmc/www/foucault1.pdf, and Hakim Bey, *T.A.Z.: The Temporary Autonomous Zone*, Autonomedia, 1991

15. 'Merkel condemns "brutal" Hamburg protests', *Financial Times*, 8
July 2017

16. https://www.handelsblatt.com/politik/international/nach-g20-treffen-
donald-trump-lobt-hamburger-polizei-und-merkel/20036954.html

17. https://www.express.co.uk/news/politics/826940/Hamburg-G20-EU-
Jean-Claude-Juncker-Merkel-resident-criticism-riots

2. THE CIRCLE OF MACHINIC ENSLAVEMENT

1. Dave Eggers, *The Circle*, Random House, 2014, p. 304
2. Peter Thiel, 'Competition is for losers', *Wall Street Journal*, 12 September 2014: https://www.wsj.com/articles/peter-thiel-competition-is-for-losers-1410535536
3. Eggers, *The Circle*, p. 390
4. https://wikileaks.org/podesta-emails/emailid/37262
5. 'Leaked: Cambridge Analytica's blueprint for Trump victory', *Guardian*, 23 March 2018: https://www.theguardian.com/uk-news/2018/mar/23/leaked-cambridge-analyticas-blueprint-for-trump-victory
6. Carole Cadwalladr, 'The great British Brexit robbery: how our democracy was hijacked', *Guardian*, 7 May 2017: https://www.theguardian.com/technology/2017/may/07/the-great-british-brexit-robbery-hijacked-democracy
7. https://www.theverge.com/2018/7/10/17556778/facebook-cambridge-analytica-fine-uk-information-commissioner
8. See Maurizio Lazzarato, 'Immaterial labour', http://www.generation-online.org/c/fcimmateriallabour3.htm
9. Maurizio Lazzarato, *Signs and Machines. Capitalism and the Production of Subjectivity*, Semiotext(e), 2014, p. 115
10. 'Computer-based personality judgments are more accurate than those made by humans', PNAS, 27 January 2015: http://www.pnas.org/content/112/4/1036
11. 'Facebook is right to think "likes" can lead to love', Bloomberg, 11 May 2018: https://www.bloomberg.com/view/articles/2018-05-11/facebook-dating-app-should-make-tinder-worry-about-its-appeal
12. Eggers, *The Circle*, p. 486
13. ' "Our minds can be hijacked": the tech insiders who fear a smartphone dystopia', *Guardian*, 6 October 2017: https://www.theguardian.com/technology/2017/oct/05/smartphone-addiction-silicon-valley-dystopia
14. 'Former Facebook executive: social media is ripping society apart', *Guardian*, 12 December 2017: https://www.theguardian.com/technology/2017/dec/11/facebook-former-executive-ripping-society-apart
15. 'Sean Parker on Facebook: "God only knows what it's doing to our children's brains" ', *The Verge*, 9 November 2017: https://www.theverge.com/2017/11/9/16627724/sean-parker-facebook-childrens-brains-feedback-loop
16. Laurent de Sutter, *Narcocapitalism*, Polity Press, 2018, p. 43

3. IT'S THE END OF THE WORLD
(AS WE KNOW IT . . .)

1. https://www.worldbank.org/en/news/press-release/2018/03/19/climate-change-could-force-over-140-million-to-migrate-within-countries-by-2050-world-bank-report

2. https://www.theguardian.com/world/2018/may/29/hungary-criminalises-migrant-helpers-stop-george-soros-legislationeur

3. https://www.google.com/search?client=safari&rls=en&q=biologists+in+France+have+stated+that+the+bird+population+in+France+has+fallen+by+a+third+over+the+last+decade+and+half.&ie=UTF-8&oe=UTF-8

4. https://www.nytimes.com/2017/07/13/magazine/seed-vault-extinction-banks-arks-of-the-apocalypse.html

5. 'Doomsday prep for the super-rich', *New Yorker*, 30 January 2017: https://www.newyorker.com/magazine/2017/01/30/doomsday-prep-for-the-super-rich

6. Ibid.

7. 'The shocking doomsday maps of the world and the billionaire escape plans', *Forbes*, 10 June 2017: https://www.forbes.com/sites/jimdobson/2017/06/10/the-shocking-doomsday-maps-of-the-world-and-the-billionaire-escape-plans/

8. Ibid.

9. Ibid.

10. https://www.whitehouse.gov/inaugural-address

11. https://forward.com/fast-forward/376842/evangelical-leaders-lay-hands-on-trump-in-oval-office/

12. All quotes are based on Antonio Spadaro and Marcelo Figueroa, 'Evangelical fundamentalism and Catholic integralism: a surprising ecumenism', *La Civiltà Cattolica*: http://www.laciviltacattolica.it/articolo/evangelical-fundamentalism-and-catholic-integralism-in-the-usa-a-surprising-ecumenism/

13. 'Silicon Valley super-rich head south to escape from a global apocalypse', *Guardian*, 29 January 2017: https://www.theguardian.com/technology/2017/jan/29/silicon-valley-new-zealand-apocalypse-escape

14. See Octave Mannoni, '*Je sais bien, mais quand même*', in *Clefs pour l'imaginaire ou l'Autre scène*, Editions du Seuil, 1968, pp. 9–33. The English translation can be found here: http://ideiaeideologia.com/wp-content/uploads/2013/05/Mannoni-I-know-very-well.pdf

15. See the work of Slavoj Žižek, who has extensively written about it

16. https://edition.cnn.com/2017/06/19/world/killer-heat-waves-rising/index.html

17. https://www.theguardian.com/environment/2018/jul/31/chinas-most-populous-area-could-be-uninhabitable-by-end-of-century

18. For a detailed explanation of the term 'slow cancellation of the future', see Franco 'Bifo' Berardi, *After the Future*, AK Press, 2011

4. THE LEFTOVERS IN EUROPE

1. See Srećko Horvat, 'The roots of this refugee crisis go back even further than the Arab Spring', *Guardian*, 24 September 2015: https://www.theguardian.com/commentisfree/2015/sep/24/refugee-crisis-arab-spring-europe-migration

2. See Roland Barthes, *Roland Barthes by Roland Barthes*, trans. by Richard Howard, University of California Press, 1994

3. See Srećko Horvat and Slavoj Žižek, *What Does Europe Want? The Union and its Discontents*, Columbia University Press, 2014

4. 'The Obama Doctrine', interview with Barack Obama by Jeffrey Goldberg, April 2016: https://www.theatlantic.com/magazine/archive/2016/04/the-obama-doctrine/471525/

5. See Saskia Sassen, *Expulsions: Brutality and the Complexity in the Global Economy*, Harvard University Press, 2014; David Harvey, *The New Imperialism*, Oxford University Press, 2003

6. See Al Jazeera documentary, *Europe's Forbidden Colony*: http://www.aljazeera.com/programmes/specialseries/2017/02/business-colonisation-170219113145085.html

7. 'Integrated reject' – a term coined by Roland Barthes: 'Perhaps there's no such thing as a community without an integrated reject. Take the world of today: very different types of societies, but probably not one without its integrated reject. All societies jealously guard their rejects, prevent them from leaving. So what would be needed as part of a globalized sociology is a theory of the incorporated reject, of the retained reject (simply: the different forms of hypocrisy, of ideological justification with regard to the pariah, who no longer tends to be recognized as such)', in Roland Barthes, *How to Live Together: Novelistic Simulations of Some Everyday Spaces*, Columbia University Press, 2013, p. 81

8. Mario Savio, Sproul Hall Steps, 2 December 1964: http://www.lib.berkeley.edu/MRC/saviotranscript.html

9. See Al Jazeera's documentary *Europe's Forbidden Colony*, Dan Davies and Srećko Horvat, 2017
10. Ibid.
11. 'Refugee children in Sweden are falling into coma-like states on learning their families will be deported', *Independent*, 1 April 2017: http://www.independent.co.uk/news/world/europe/refugee-children-sweden-coma-like-states-families-deported-uppgivenhetssyndrom-resignation-syndrome-a7662126.html

5. MAKE MARGARET ATWOOD FICTION AGAIN!

1. All quotes from Imre Kertész, *Fatelessness*, Vintage, 2004
2. Margaret Atwood, 'What "The Handmaid's Tale" means in the age of Trump', *New York Times*, 10 March 2017
3. https://www.cbsnews.com/news/us-drops-mother-of-all-bombs-in-afghanistan-marking-weapons-first-use/
4. Atwood, 'What "The Handmaid's Tale" means in the age of Trump'

INTERLUDE: AUSCHWITZ ON THE BEACH?

1. 'Refugees suffering "Auschwitz on the Beach"? Germans say No', *New York Times*, 23 August 2017: https://www.nytimes.com/2017/08/23/arts/auschwitz-on-the-beach-documenta-14-controversy.html
2. Imre Kertész, 'Who owns Auschwitz?', *The Yale Journal of Criticism*, Volume 14, Number 1, Spring 2001, pp. 267–72
3. Ibid.
4. Ibid.
5. See J. L. Austin, *How to Do Things with Words*, Harvard University Press, 2nd edn, 1975
6. See 'world system theory' and the works of Immanuel Wallerstein, Giovanni Arrighi and Samir Amin among others
7. The whole conversation can be found in my book published in Croatian, *Pažnja neprijatelj prisluškuje!*, Ljevak, 2011, a collection of interviews with Amos Oz, Francis Fukuyama, Slavoj Žižek, Philip Zimbardo, Terry Eagleton, Gayatri Spivak, Zygmunt Bauman and others
8. Walter Benjamin, *Illuminations: Essays and Reflections*, ed. Hannah Arendt, trans. Henry Zohn, 1968; Schocken Books, 2007, p. 258

6. SUMMER IN ATHENS:
HOPE WITHOUT OPTIMISM

1. See Srećko Horvat and Slavoj Žižek, *What Does Europe Want?*, Columbia University Press, 2014
2. See 'IMF: Austerity measures would still leave Greece with unsustainable debt', *Guardian*, 30 June 2015: https://www.theguardian.com/business/2015/jun/30/greek-debt-troika-analysis-says-significant-concessions-still-needed
3. 'Greece debt crisis: IMF payment missed as bailout expires', BBC, 1 July 2015: http://www.bbc.com/news/world-europe-33339363
4. http://uk.businessinsider.com/greeces-finance-minister-yanis-varoufakis-waterboarding-cia-troika-bailout-2015-2
5. See Yanis Varoufakis, *Adults in the Room*, Penguin, 2017
6. 'Greece Debt Crisis: Alexis Tsipras is an author of Greek tragedy, says Wikipedia', *Independent*, 7 July 2015: http://www.independent.co.uk/life-style/gadgets-and-tech/news/greece-debt-crisis-alexis-tsipras-is-an-author-of-greek-tragedy-says-wikipedia-10372183.html
7. See Walter Benjamin, 'Left-Wing Melancholy: On Erich Kästner's new book of poems', *Screen*, Volume 15, Issue 2, 1 July 1974, 28–32
8. Enzo Traverso, *Left-Wing Melancholia: Marxism, History, and Memory*, Columbia University Press, 2016, p. 45
9. See Wendy Brown, 'Resisting Left Melancholy', *boundary* 2, Duke University Press, Volume 26, Number 3, Fall 1999
10. Traverso, *Left-Wing Melancholia*, p. 45
11. Rosa Luxemburg, 'Order prevails in Berlin', January 1919, online version: https://www.marxists.org/archive/luxemburg/1919/01/14.htm
12. Transcript of the whole conversation available in Croatian, published in *Jutarnji List*: http://www.jutarnji.hr/vijesti/svijet/slavni-intelektualac-ekskluzivno-za-jutarnji-ako-se-europska-unija-raspadne-vratit-cemo-se-svijetu-koji-nema-puno-sanse-za-opstanak/5117288/
13. Terry Eagleton, *Hope Without Optimism*, University of Virginia Press, 2015, p. 52
14. See Slavoj Žižek, *The Courage of Hopelessness*, Penguin, 2017
15. Eagleton, *Hope Without Optimism*, p. 132

7. ISLANDS OUTSIDE CAPITALISM?

1. For more information see George Dafermos, 'The Catalan Integral Cooperative: An Organizational Study of a Post-Capitalist Cooperative':

http://commonstransition.org/the-catalan-integral-cooperative-an-organizational-study-of-a-post-capitalist-cooperative/

2. For more about Enric Durán and his connection to the CIC see: 'On the lam with bank robber Enric Durán', VICE, 6 April 2015: https://www.vice.com/en_us/article/wd7edm/be-the-bank-you-want-to-see-in-the-world-0000626-v22n4

3. 'Tarnac "anarchist cell" on trial in France over 2008 suspected rail sabotage': http://www.france24.com/en/20180313-france-tarnac-anarchist-cell-trial-france-over-2008-suspected-tgv-rail-sabotage

4. 'Leftwing "anarchist terror cell" is fiction, French judges rule', *Guardian*, 13 April 2018: https://www.theguardian.com/world/2018/apr/13/tarnac-nine-leftwing-anarchist-terror-cell-fiction-france

5. Giorgio Agamben, '*Terrorisme ou tragi-comédie*', *Libération*, 19 November 2008

6. The Invisible Committee, *The Coming Insurrection*, Semiotext(e), 2009, p. 88

7. The Invisible Committee, *Now*, Semiotext(e), 2017

8. See Benedict Anderson's seminal book *Imagined Communities*, Verso, 1983

8. *MAMMA MIA!* THERE ARE NO ISLANDS ANY MORE

1. Franz Kafka, *The Burrow and Other Stories*, Penguin, 2017, p. 122

2. 'The film-makers' location of choice', *The Times*, 11 August 2017: https://www.thetimes.co.uk/article/the-film-makers-location-of-choice-dnok3nrgq

3. 'Mamma Mia! How the feelgood movie of 2008 has ruined the Greek paradise island of Skopelos', *Daily Mail*, 31 July 2009, online: http://www.dailymail.co.uk/femail/article-1203536/Mamma-Mia-How-feelgood-movie-2008-ruined-Greek-paradise-island-Skopelos.html

4. Philipp Bouhler (ed.), *Der grossdeutsche Freiheitskampf. Reden Adolf Hitlers vom 1 September 1939 bis 10 März 1940*, Zentralverlag der NSDAP, Franz Eher Nachfolger, 1940, p. 67; Henry Picker, *Hitlers Tischgespräche im Führerhauptquartier*, Seewald, 1977, S. 69 (8.9.1941)

5. All exchanges between Churchill and Fitzroy Maclean are quoted from Fitzroy Maclean, *Eastern Approaches*, Penguin, 2009

6. Ibid., p. 303

7. Ibid., pp. 315–16
8. Ibid., pp. 329–30
9. Ibid., pp. 402–3

9. FOR A GLOBAL LIBERATION MOVEMENT

1. 'Southern mayors defy Italian coalition to offer safe port to migrants', *Guardian*, 11 June 2018: https://www.theguardian.com/world/2018/jun/10/italy-shuts-ports-to-rescue-boat-with-629-migrants-on-board
2. 'Forced displacement at record 68.5 million', UNHCR, 19 June 2018: http://www.unhcr.org/news/stories/2018/6/5b222c494/forced-displacement-record-685-million.html
3. Tariq Ali, *The Extreme Centre: A Warning*, Verso, 2015

10. POETRY FROM THE FUTURE

1. Karl Marx, *The Eighteenth Brumaire of Louis Bonaparte*, in *Surveys from Exile*, trans. P. Jackson, Penguin, 1973, p. 149
2. Étienne Balibar, *The Philosophy of Marx*, Verso, 1995, p. 40
3. Walter Benjamin, *Illuminations: Essays and Reflections*, ed. Hannah Arendt, trans. Henry Zohn, 1968; Schocken Books, 2007, p. 262
4. For further elaboration of this point see Louis Althusser, *Machiavelli and Us*, Verso, 2011, p. 50
5. Benjamin, *Illuminations*, p. 261
6. Enzo Traverso, *Left-Wing Melancholia*, Columbia University Press, 2016, p. 8
7. Étienne Balibar, 'The Idea of Revolution: Yesterday, Today and Tomorrow': http://blogs.law.columbia.edu/uprising1313/etienne-balibar-the-idea-of-revolution-yesterday-today-and-tomorrow/
8. Alenka Zupančič, 'The apocalypse is disappointing', unpublished manuscript
9. Ibid.
10. 'Trump tosses paper towels into Puerto Rico crowd', CNN, 3 October 2017
11. Marx's original phrase, *'Poesie aus der Zukunft'* ('poetry from the future'), is from *The Eighteenth Brumaire*, 1852
12. The anecdote is based on Jen Couch, 'Imagining Zapatismo', *Communal/Plural*, 9 (2), 2001, p. 249

13. Subcomandante Galeano, 'Prelude: Timepieces, the Apocalypse, and the Hour of the Small', 12 April 2017: http://enlacezapatista.ezln.org.mx/2017/04/24/prelude-timepieces-the-apocalypse-and-the-hour-of-the-smallsubcomandante-insurgente-galeano/

14. Ibid.

15. Ibid.

Soundtrack –
There Is No Liberation
without Music

Anouar Brahem – *Conte de l'incroyable amour*
Bertolt Brecht – *An die Nachgeborenen* (1939 recording)
Dubravka Jusić – *El Shatt*
Rade Šerbedžija and Vanessa Redgrave – *Moj brat*
Đorđe Balašević – *Računajte na nas*
Timber Timbre – *Western Questions*
Кино – *Кончится лето*
Cigarettes After Sex – *Apocalypse*
Darko Rundek – *Apokalipso*
Ali Fara Touré and Toumani – *Diabate*
Tiken Jah Fakoly – *Dernier Appel*
Klaus Kinski – *Geheimnis der Jugend*
The Radio Department – *Sloboda Narodu*
Rani Mraz – *Triput sam video Tita*
Leonard Cohen – *The Partisan*
Μικρόκοσμος-Ν.Χικμέτ- Θ.Μικρούτσικος- Μ.Δημητριάδη
Miki Trifunov – *Pjesma o zavođenju*
Daleka Obala – *Sušac Blues*
Valentino Bošković – *Adeyata*
Refused – *New Noise*

Acknowledgements –
There Is No Book without
Comrades

My name is Legion, for we are many
(Mark 5:9)

There is no book with a single author and without the voices of others. Among the Legion, without whom this and many other endeavours wouldn't be possible, are my comrades in arms, theory and hope: Noam Chomsky, Yanis Varoufakis, Slavoj Žižek, Aleksandra Savanović, Renata Avila, Julian Assange, Alfonso Cuarón, Alenka Zupančič, Franco 'Bifo' Berardi, Samir Amin, Tariq Ali, Jelena Ostojić, Marko Pogačar, Jovica Lončar, Stéphane Hessel, Antonio Negri, Mladen Dolar, Michael Hardt, Saskia Sassen, Andrej Nikolaidis, Nikola Devčić-Mišo, Angela Richter, Maja Pelević, Sarah Harrison, Tonči Valentić, Boris Buden, Vedran Horvat, Nadežda Čačinovič, Igor Bezinovič, Sebastian Kaiser, Laurent de Sutter, Karl-Heinz Dellwo, Gabriele Rollnik, Ivan Ergić, Paul Mason, Maja Kantar, Vedran Velagić, Ivana Biočina, Slobodan Velikić, Pliketi Plok, Filip Balunović and numerous others whose thoughts and experience were invaluable to me during the last decade and will be in the decades to come. Many points in this book, even if we didn't always agree on everything, took shape precisely during our numerous discussions led by pure curiosity and the joy of imagining – and changing – the world. Not only the early days of the student occupations in Croatia (2009) and the organizing of the Subversive Festival in Zagreb (2008–13), but also the thinking and writing process with my co-author Igor Štiks led to two previous books which were laying the foundations for this book itself: *Pravo na pobunu* ('Right to Rebellion', in Croatian, Fraktura, 2010) and the edited volume *Welcome to the Desert of Post-Socialism. Radical Politics After Yugoslavia* (Verso, 2014). For a better understanding of the Yugoslav Liberation Movement (NOB) and the Non-Aligned Movement, I owe my gratitude to Budimir Lončar, last serving minister of foreign affairs of Yugoslavia (1987–91) and one of the last big diplomats of the twentieth century, whose memory and insights remain a true source of inspiration for imagining a non-aligned geopolitics in the twenty-first century. This endeavour would probably look completely different if there wasn't the roller-coaster ride through Europe with Dan Davies and Anson Hartford when making our Al Jazeera documentary *Europe's Forbidden Colony* (2017), and all the people – from activists to refugees – whom we met on our never-ending tour. Nor would it have the same impetus and sense of urgency if there wasn't the roller-coaster ride of the Democracy in Europe Movement (DiEM25) and the politics of friendship and hope without optimism that binds us together and knows no borders. There is nothing without the generosity and openness of others; this book – and many other more important things – wouldn't be possible without Sandra Vitaljić. Books are also not possible without those who are usually in the shadow – if there wasn't my editor Thomas Penn, who coincidentally or not called me and invited me to write a book for Penguin precisely when I was on the island of Vis in April 2016, avoiding any new calls and invitations, who knows whether it would have ever seen the light of day. His comments and patient edits added more clarity and precision to *Poetry from the Future*. This book would definitely have less of the poetry – and even less of a hope – without the delicious food, wine and *rakija* shared with Kajo, Čedo, Senko Karuza and many others from the island of Vis, thanks to whose lives and generosity I came to understand better what *pomalo* truly means. Last but not least, there is no poetry from the future, no single sentence and no hope, without the radicality of love named Saša.

Index

ALLEN LANE
an imprint of
PENGUIN BOOKS

Also Published

Stuart Russell, *Human Compatible: AI and the Problem of Control*

Serhii Plokhy, *Forgotten Bastards of the Eastern Front: An Untold Story of World War II*

Dominic Sandbrook, *Who Dares Wins: Britain, 1979-1982*

Charles Moore, *Margaret Thatcher: The Authorized Biography, Volume Three: Herself Alone*

Thomas Penn, *The Brothers York: An English Tragedy*

David Abulafia, *The Boundless Sea: A Human History of the Oceans*

Anthony Aguirre, *Cosmological Koans: A Journey to the Heart of Physics*

Orlando Figes, *The Europeans: Three Lives and the Making of a Cosmopolitan Culture*

Naomi Klein, *On Fire: The Burning Case for a Green New Deal*

Anne Boyer, *The Undying: A Meditation on Modern Illness*

Benjamin Moser, *Sontag: Her Life*

Daniel Markovits, *The Meritocracy Trap*

Malcolm Gladwell, *Talking to Strangers: What We Should Know about the People We Don't Know*

Peter Hennessy, *Winds of Change: Britain in the Early Sixties*

John Sellars, *Lessons in Stoicism: What Ancient Philosophers Teach Us about How to Live*

Brendan Simms, *Hitler: Only the World Was Enough*

Hassan Damluji, *The Responsible Globalist: What Citizens of the World Can Learn from Nationalism*

Peter Gatrell, *The Unsettling of Europe: The Great Migration, 1945 to the Present*

Justin Marozzi, *Islamic Empires: Fifteen Cities that Define a Civilization*

Bruce Hood, *Possessed: Why We Want More Than We Need*

Susan Neiman, *Learning from the Germans: Confronting Race and the Memory of Evil*

Donald D. Hoffman, *The Case Against Reality: How Evolution Hid the Truth from Our Eyes*

Frank Close, *Trinity: The Treachery and Pursuit of the Most Dangerous Spy in History*

Richard M. Eaton, *India in the Persianate Age: 1000-1765*

Janet L. Nelson, *King and Emperor: A New Life of Charlemagne*

Philip Mansel, *King of the World: The Life of Louis XIV*

Donald Sassoon, *The Anxious Triumph: A Global History of Capitalism, 1860-1914*

Elliot Ackerman, *Places and Names: On War, Revolution and Returning*

Jonathan Aldred, *Licence to be Bad: How Economics Corrupted Us*

Johny Pitts, *Afropean: Notes from Black Europe*

Walt Odets, *Out of the Shadows: Reimagining Gay Men's Lives*

James Lovelock, *Novacene: The Coming Age of Hyperintelligence*

Mark B. Smith, *The Russia Anxiety: And How History Can Resolve It*

Stella Tillyard, *George IV: King in Waiting*

Jonathan Rée, *Witcraft: The Invention of Philosophy in English*

Jared Diamond, *Upheaval: How Nations Cope with Crisis and Change*

Emma Dabiri, *Don't Touch My Hair*

Srecko Horvat, *Poetry from the Future: Why a Global Liberation Movement Is Our Civilisation's Last Chance*

Paul Mason, *Clear Bright Future: A Radical Defence of the Human Being*

Remo H. Largo, *The Right Life: Human Individuality and its role in our development, health and happiness*

Joseph Stiglitz, *People, Power and Profits: Progressive Capitalism for an Age of Discontent*

David Brooks, *The Second Mountain*

Roberto Calasso, *The Unnamable Present*

Lee Smolin, *Einstein's Unfinished Revolution: The Search for What Lies Beyond the Quantum*

Clare Carlisle, *Philosopher of the Heart: The Restless Life of Søren Kierkegaard*

Nicci Gerrard, *What Dementia Teaches Us About Love*

Edward O. Wilson, *Genesis: On the Deep Origin of Societies*

John Barton, *A History of the Bible: The Book and its Faiths*

Carolyn Forché, *What You Have Heard is True: A Memoir of Witness and Resistance*

Elizabeth-Jane Burnett, *The Grassling*

Kate Brown, *Manual for Survival: A Chernobyl Guide to the Future*

Roderick Beaton, *Greece: Biography of a Modern Nation*

Matt Parker, *Humble Pi: A Comedy of Maths Errors*

Ruchir Sharma, *Democracy on the Road*

David Wallace-Wells, *The Uninhabitable Earth: A Story of the Future*

Randolph M. Nesse, *Good Reasons for Bad Feelings: Insights from the Frontier of Evolutionary Psychiatry*

Anand Giridharadas, *Winners Take All: The Elite Charade of Changing the World*

Richard Bassett, *Last Days in Old Europe: Triste '79, Vienna '85, Prague '89*

Paul Davies, *The Demon in the Machine: How Hidden Webs of Information Are Finally Solving the Mystery of Life*

Toby Green, *A Fistful of Shells: West Africa from the Rise of the Slave Trade to the Age of Revolution*

Paul Dolan, *Happy Ever After: Escaping the Myth of The Perfect Life*

Sunil Amrith, *Unruly Waters: How Mountain Rivers and Monsoons Have Shaped South Asia's History*

Christopher Harding, *Japan Story: In Search of a Nation, 1850 to the Present*

Timothy Day, *I Saw Eternity the Other Night: King's College, Cambridge, and an English Singing Style*

Richard Abels, *Aethelred the Unready: The Failed King*

Eric Kaufmann, *Whiteshift: Populism, Immigration and the Future of White Majorities*

Alan Greenspan and Adrian Wooldridge, *Capitalism in America: A History*

Philip Hensher, *The Penguin Book of the Contemporary British Short Story*

Paul Collier, *The Future of Capitalism: Facing the New Anxieties*

Andrew Roberts, *Churchill: Walking With Destiny*

Tim Flannery, *Europe: A Natural History*

T. M. Devine, *The Scottish Clearances: A History of the Dispossessed, 1600-1900*

Robert Plomin, *Blueprint: How DNA Makes Us Who We Are*

Michael Lewis, *The Fifth Risk: Undoing Democracy*

Diarmaid MacCulloch, *Thomas Cromwell: A Life*

Ramachandra Guha, *Gandhi: 1914-1948*

Slavoj Žižek, *Like a Thief in Broad Daylight: Power in the Era of Post-Humanity*

Neil MacGregor, *Living with the Gods: On Beliefs and Peoples*

Peter Biskind, *The Sky is Falling: How Vampires, Zombies, Androids and Superheroes Made America Great for Extremism*

Robert Skidelsky, *Money and Government: A Challenge to Mainstream Economics*

Helen Parr, *Our Boys: The Story of a Paratrooper*

David Gilmour, *The British in India: Three Centuries of Ambition and Experience*

Jonathan Haidt and Greg Lukianoff, *The Coddling of the American Mind: How Good Intentions and Bad Ideas are Setting up a Generation for Failure*

Ian Kershaw, *Roller-Coaster: Europe, 1950-2017*

Adam Tooze, *Crashed: How a Decade of Financial Crises Changed the World*

Edmund King, *Henry I: The Father of His People*

Lilia M. Schwarcz and Heloisa M. Starling, *Brazil: A Biography*

Jesse Norman, *Adam Smith: What He Thought, and Why it Matters*

Philip Augur, *The Bank that Lived a Little: Barclays in the Age of the Very Free Market*

Christopher Andrew, *The Secret World: A History of Intelligence*

David Edgerton, *The Rise and Fall of the British Nation: A Twentieth-Century History*

Julian Jackson, *A Certain Idea of France: The Life of Charles de Gaulle*

Owen Hatherley, *Trans-Europe Express*

Richard Wilkinson and Kate Pickett, *The Inner Level: How More Equal Societies Reduce Stress, Restore Sanity and Improve Everyone's Wellbeing*

Paul Kildea, *Chopin's Piano: A Journey Through Romanticism*

Seymour M. Hersh, *Reporter: A Memoir*

Michael Pollan, *How to Change Your Mind: The New Science of Psychedelics*

David Christian, *Origin Story: A Big History of Everything*

Judea Pearl and Dana Mackenzie, *The Book of Why: The New Science of Cause and Effect*

David Graeber, *Bullshit Jobs: A Theory*

Serhii Plokhy, *Chernobyl: History of a Tragedy*

Michael McFaul, *From Cold War to Hot Peace: The Inside Story of Russia and America*

Paul Broks, *The Darker the Night, the Brighter the Stars: A Neuropsychologist's Odyssey*

Lawrence Wright, *God Save Texas: A Journey into the Future of America*

John Gray, *Seven Types of Atheism*

Carlo Rovelli, *The Order of Time*

Mariana Mazzucato, *The Value of Everything: Making and Taking in the Global Economy*

Richard Vinen, *The Long '68: Radical Protest and Its Enemies*

Kishore Mahbubani, *Has the West Lost It?: A Provocation*

John Lewis Gaddis, *On Grand Strategy*

Richard Overy, *The Birth of the RAF, 1918: The World's First Air Force*

Francis Pryor, *Paths to the Past: Encounters with Britain's Hidden Landscapes*

Helen Castor, *Elizabeth I: A Study in Insecurity*

Ken Robinson and Lou Aronica, *You, Your Child and School*

Leonard Mlodinow, *Elastic: Flexible Thinking in a Constantly Changing World*

Nick Chater, *The Mind is Flat: The Illusion of Mental Depth and The Improvised Mind*

Michio Kaku, *The Future of Humanity: Terraforming Mars, Interstellar Travel, Immortality, and Our Destiny Beyond*

Thomas Asbridge, *Richard I: The Crusader King*

Richard Sennett, *Building and Dwelling: Ethics for the City*

Nassim Nicholas Taleb, *Skin in the Game: Hidden Asymmetries in Daily Life*

Steven Pinker, *Enlightenment Now: The Case for Reason, Science, Humanism and Progress*

Steve Coll, *Directorate S: The C.I.A. and America's Secret Wars in Afghanistan, 2001 - 2006*

Jordan B. Peterson, *12 Rules for Life: An Antidote to Chaos*

Bruno Maçães, *The Dawn of Eurasia: On the Trail of the New World Order*

Brock Bastian, *The Other Side of Happiness: Embracing a More Fearless Approach to Living*

Ryan Lavelle, *Cnut: The North Sea King*

Tim Blanning, *George I: The Lucky King*

Thomas Cogswell, *James I: The Phoenix King*

Pete Souza, *Obama, An Intimate Portrait: The Historic Presidency in Photographs*

Robert Dallek, *Franklin D. Roosevelt: A Political Life*

Norman Davies, *Beneath Another Sky: A Global Journey into History*

Ian Black, *Enemies and Neighbours: Arabs and Jews in Palestine and Israel, 1917-2017*

Martin Goodman, *A History of Judaism*

Shami Chakrabarti, *Of Women: In the 21st Century*

Stephen Kotkin, *Stalin, Vol. II: Waiting for Hitler, 1928-1941*

Lindsey Fitzharris, *The Butchering Art: Joseph Lister's Quest to Transform the Grisly World of Victorian Medicine*

Serhii Plokhy, *Lost Kingdom: A History of Russian Nationalism from Ivan the Great to Vladimir Putin*

Mark Mazower, *What You Did Not Tell: A Russian Past and the Journey Home*

Lawrence Freedman, *The Future of War: A History*

Niall Ferguson, *The Square and the Tower: Networks, Hierarchies and the Struggle for Global Power*

Matthew Walker, *Why We Sleep: The New Science of Sleep and Dreams*

Edward O. Wilson, *The Origins of Creativity*

John Bradshaw, *The Animals Among Us: The New Science of Anthropology*

David Cannadine, *Victorious Century: The United Kingdom, 1800-1906*

Leonard Susskind and Art Friedman, *Special Relativity and Classical Field Theory*

Maria Alyokhina, *Riot Days*

Oona A. Hathaway and Scott J. Shapiro, *The Internationalists: And Their Plan to Outlaw War*

Chris Renwick, *Bread for All: The Origins of the Welfare State*

Anne Applebaum, *Red Famine: Stalin's War on Ukraine*

Richard McGregor, *Asia's Reckoning: The Struggle for Global Dominance*

Chris Kraus, *After Kathy Acker: A Biography*

Clair Wills, *Lovers and Strangers: An Immigrant History of Post-War Britain*

Odd Arne Westad, *The Cold War: A World History*

Max Tegmark, *Life 3.0: Being Human in the Age of Artificial Intelligence*

Jonathan Losos, *Improbable Destinies: How Predictable is Evolution?*

Chris D. Thomas, *Inheritors of the Earth: How Nature Is Thriving in an Age of Extinction*